THE HARD WORK MYTH

By Barnaby Lashbrooke

Published by Time etc

All enquiries to myth@timeetc.com

First published 2019

ISBN 978-1-5272-5070-3

ACKNOWLEDGMENTS

I talk a lot in this book about what I've achieved, but the truth is none of it would have been possible without the amazing team I work with at Time etc's headquarters, the incredible clients we support or the hundreds of talented Virtual Assistants we work with. Thank you.

To Emily for your incredible work on this book, putting up with all the edits and sticking with it until the very end.

To Penni for being such an inspiration to me.

Thanks to my Virtual Assistant, Lisa, for saving me from my inbox in a world of 'infobesity'.

For my amazing kids Maisy and Harry for being two incredible reasons not to spend my life working.

For my partner Kirst for always believing in me and encouraging me every step of the way. I couldn't do it without you.

To Lynne, David, Kirsty, Ben, Sam and Fran for supporting me and helping shape who I am.

ABOUT THE AUTHOR

Barnaby Lashbrooke is an entrepreneur and investor. By day, he is CEO of virtual assistant service Time Etc, a job he loves, but to which he strictly devotes just 35-hours a week.

After suffering from crippling burnout for years, which damaged his mental and physical health, affected his personal relationships and threatened to derail his business, Barnaby realized he needed to make some dramatic changes in his life.

By studying the habits of some of the world's most successful people, and learning about the psychology behind productivity, Barnaby worked out how to work less and achieve more, which he reveals in *The Hard Work Myth*.

His journey gave him a new respect for time and turned his flailing startup business into a multi-million-dollar enterprise operating in the U.K. and U.S.

Most importantly, it freed him up to spend more quality time with his two favorite people, his kids Maisy and Harry.

CHAPTERS

INTRODUCTION

I'm in the bottom 19% of entrepreneurs and it's one of my greatest achievements.

Yes, you read that right. My 35-hour work week puts me well and truly at the bottom of the entrepreneur league tables, while almost half (49%) of entrepreneurs work 50+ hours a week[1].

When people learn about the hours I work, they often assume I'm running some sort of lifestyle business, the kind that ticks-over in the background and makes me just enough money to enjoy myself.

But they'd be wrong. Since I've been working a 35-hour week my business has grown from less than $1million in revenue to almost eight figures and is generating multi-million-dollar profits.

---

[1]According to a study of entrepreneurs' working hours by The Alternative Board

Why do people make this assumption? It's called The Hard Work Myth: the widely held belief that the way you achieve success and financial freedom is by working harder... and harder.

Many of us believe in The Hard Work Myth, despite proving to ourselves time and time again, throughout our lives, that hard work alone very rarely ever equals huge success.

I'm not the only one who's figured this out. When I studied some of the world's most successful business leaders, including Oprah Winfrey, Sir Richard Branson, Jeff Bezos, Ariana Huffington, Bill Gates and Warren Buffet, it became clear to me they don't buy it either. And, yet, the myth perpetuates.

The Hard Work Myth is the single biggest cause of millions of the world's brightest and most capable people sacrificing more of their lives than they need to in the pursuit of success.

The truth is you already have everything you need for success. You are already infinitely capable of achieving everything you could possibly wish for.

Once you've read *The Hard Work Myth*, my hope is that you will give yourself permission to stop thrashing yourself in an effort to achieve more, when this kind of behavior is far more likely to be holding you back.

But first, I'd like to take you back a few years, because I didn't always work 35-hours a week.

Why I wrote this book

This time a decade ago, it's likely you would have found me watching daytime television repeats in bed during working hours. To me, that seemed preferable to going into the office.

On paper, I was successful. My entrepreneurial exploits began aged 17 making websites for friends' bands and, with the internet booming, this had quickly expanded into selling domain names and hosting to the masses. Before I knew it, I'd created a company with 24,000 customers from my bedroom on a computer I built myself.

Six years later, I sold the business and did what many 24-year-olds might have done, bought a top floor apartment and a Ferrari and set about plotting my next big move.

Riding high on my success, it wasn't long before I started business number two, which I believed would be as straightforward as the first.

The vision was to build a network of skilled, experienced and carefully-vetted virtual assistants that time-poor entrepreneurs could hire by the hour to perform administrative tasks, saving them hours of time and freeing them up to achieve more.

I knew there was a market for this because I had been desperate for this kind of support when I was building my first business. For years, it had been just me, on my own, wearing lots of different hats. Sales one minute, technical support the next and admin when I could squeeze it in. I had longed for someone to take on some of the things I didn't have time to do, or hated doing.

My early success had made me confident. As a young millionaire I told people how fast I expected this new company would grow as I set about building a website, hiring staff and finding our first few customers, just as I had done before.

But almost as soon as I'd started the business, things began to get difficult. For reasons I couldn't fathom, we struggled to find customers and our workers kept leaving. Month after month we hemorrhaged money.

Every day was like trying to run up a sand dune. I was confronted with a hundred different problems that I didn't have answers to. All I could think of to do was keep on running as the sand slipped beneath my feet. The result? All my passion and enthusiasm drained away.

In those early years, I never felt on top of things. I didn't matter how many hours I worked or how many things I ticked off my to-do list every day, I couldn't even keep the wheels on, let alone find the time to develop into the leader I knew I was capable of being.

And fear was crippling me. I was terrified I would never get the business to profitability, that I would fail and have to start over, that I could be treading water for years and have nothing to show for it.

At the office, I physically and mentally shut the door. Eventually, I became so unapproachable I figured I should work from home. In the company I was trying to lead and grow, I would make an appearance a couple of days a week.

I had no trust in anyone and no one trusted me either, which made employee retention even more of a challenge.

My own output was low. Without deadlines I procrastinated, which I hated. To compensate I'd work longer hours, in an effort to salvage each day that went by. I'd numb my sense of failure by drinking every night, which made mornings a struggle.

Then, in 2011, my mother died after a four-year battle with cancer. She lived for her children, long after we had grown up and flown the nest. When she passed away, I felt isolated, as well as devastated. I lost the emotional support she had given us so freely, and that I had long used as a crutch. We had talked a lot about the business, and she had often talked me down off the edge.

In the months following her death, as I wrestled with the grief and pain, I started to re-evaluate my life. Realizing how short it can be, I started looking at what worked and what didn't.

And then, on a sunny Tuesday in May, when I was at my lowest ebb, I had an epiphany while driving my car.

It probably saved my life.

I realized the way I had been trying to succeed was flawed. My tactic was that if I worked all the hours possible, everything would somehow slot into place. It hadn't worked.

Worse still, I realized that working harder had actually put me further away from the success I so desperately wanted.

That moment changed my life forever.

I started to view time as the most precious commodity of all.

After that epiphany, I would spend years researching techniques on how to achieve more in less time, conducting experiments on myself to find the breakthroughs that would really work. I hacked my own psychology and inverted the way I think about work and success.

Instead of forcing myself to work fruitlessly on my ailing business, I applied myself to becoming an expert in achieving more while working less hard. For the first time in years, things started looking up.

That self-transformation would also transform my business, Time Etc, from an abject failure into a global success story, which is now fast approaching total sales of more than $35 million. The business has achieved its purpose and changed the lives of thousands of entrepreneurs and professionals by liberating them from more than two million tasks, saving them half a million hours to spend with their families or growing their businesses.

Our company has won multiple awards, is ranked as a top 1% business worldwide for employee engagement by Gallup, has enjoyed one of the very highest Glassdoor ratings possible and received hundreds of five-star reviews from happy customers.

Better still, my life working 100-hours a week is over. I no longer live in a permanently burned-out state and my business is growing. Most of my spare time is spent having fun with my daughter Maisy and my son Harry.

I wrote this book because I see so many entrepreneurs struggling to achieve success by working themselves to the bone.

I've seen too many talented people fall for The Hard Work Myth, only to end up feeling tired, empty and drained, rather than fulfilled, successful and satisfied.

I care passionately about helping business owners to avoid the hell I went through for several years.

My message to you is simple: the power to achieve more is within you already and it has *nothing* to do with working longer hours.

You can take control of your future by gaining a higher level of awareness about why you are repeating senseless habits.

If you're suspicious that a person you've never heard of is telling you it's possible to achieve more and work less hard, I understand, and I will endeavor to win you over in the forthcoming chapters.

But what you should be more suspicious of is our capitalist system which promotes a whopper of a lie that is damaging to our mental and physical health.

In pre-school they start teaching us that the harder we work, the more successful we'll be. In our teens we're told that the longer we sit in front of our books, the better we'll do in our exams. And the way our education system works, that's more or less true, so it's no surprise that we all end up believing it. But real life is nothing like school.

What to expect from this book

What you won't find in this book are complex theoretical techniques devised by clever experts on time management. You won't find comparisons between entrepreneurs and world-class athletes with suggestions on how you can copy their approach to training, work and diet to get ahead. You won't find revelations from real high performers about getting up at 4am and partaking in cryotherapy before heading to the office with a murky green juice.

Instead you'll find suggested changes that you can start making today to achieve more, without working harder, designed specifically for normal people like us who are juggling life with growing a business.

I'm neither a guru nor a self-help expert. I'm just an ordinary business owner, like you, sharing techniques that have been refined, tested and proven over the last 20 years.

This might not be the book you think it is. There are no productivity hacks or shortcuts. Instead, it will force you to question yourself, change how you think and approach tasks and hurdles. It will cause you to analyze your attitude to time and how and why you waste it every day. And it will help you gain a new level of awareness that will help you get more out of every minute you devote to work.

I may not work many hours each week, but I am laser-focused, disciplined, passionate, hard-working and extremely committed during the hours that I do work.

If this book does one thing, I hope it will help you realize the damaging effects of thrashing yourself and help you understand how much your own productivity is linked to your happiness.

Who is this book for?

If you have found this book, I already know three things about you:

1. You're a hard-working entrepreneur, freelancer or leader who calls the shots on your time.

2. You know you want to achieve more but you don't know how other than to work even harder. An unproductive day means you will sit at your desk for another hour or use weekends to play catch up. You write unachievable to-do lists and feel guilty when you don't cross everything off.
3. There is someone in your life to whom you are not giving enough time. Is it a child, a partner, a parent, or you?

You are reading this because you know how it feels when those bursts of productivity take hold: it's like you can conquer the world, or just get home to enjoy the simple pleasure of reading your children a bedtime story. You want more days to feel like that.

You are reading this because you worry that in 10 years' time you'll be in exactly the same position as you are now.

But you are not alone and, by contemplating what you read in this book, you will realize the things that are holding you back are the very same things that plague us all.

I hope this book helps you achieve everything that you're capable of.

CHAPTER ONE

WORKING HARDER IS FAILING YOU

"Hard work never killed anybody, but why take a chance?"
– *Edgar Bergen*

I want to tell you a story about a guy called Jeff. Back in 1994, Jeff left the long-hours of a highly paid corporate career on Wall Street to start his own business.

But Jeff doesn't like to work too hard. He goes to bed early, gets eight hours' sleep and, after waking up, likes to "putter" a while, enjoying his morning coffee, reading the newspaper, cooking big breakfasts and hanging out with his kids before they go to school.

After breakfast, he does the dishes before starting work at 10am.

Jeff realized a few years ago that he works best in the mornings, so he likes to get any "high IQ" meetings done and dusted before lunchtime. Jeff is well aware that, due to decision fatigue, making good choices gets harder throughout the day so, by 5pm, he'll postpone any decision making until 10am the next day.

Try to picture Jeff, and you might think of a relaxed entrepreneur, with plenty of time for his friends and family, perhaps running a lifestyle business or small consultancy.

It's unlikely you'll have pictured Jeff Bezos[2], the founder and CEO of Amazon who, at the time of writing, has built a $233 billion revenue business and a personal net worth of $153.5 billion.

If Jeff Bezos can make billions *and* enjoy his life, why are you sacrificing so much?

What are you sacrificing in the pursuit of success?

I'm going to bet that, since you've been working for yourself, you've sacrificed at least one of these:

- Evenings
- Vacations

---

[2] Jeff Bezos' daily routine, as reported by CNBC

- Work-free weekends
- Sleeping for long enough to feel fully rested
- Keeping vaguely-normal working hours

I'm also going to bet that, when you do take a break from work, you find yourself checking emails, reaching for your phone or thinking about things you need to do on your return.

The truth is that not knowing when to stop is an endemic problem for high-achieving people. Working long hours is a badge of honor, and it even earns you empathy and camaraderie from your peers. Jokes about having no work-life balance are parodied by the entrepreneurial community:

"I'll sleep when I die!"
"Weekend, what weekend?!"

Working long hours is widely accepted to be part of the crazy, anti-social life of an entrepreneur who hopes that putting in the hard yards now means retirement at 45 years old.

Few of us question this because, from our very first day at school, we are heavily influenced to accept hard work as a required component of success.

But the truth about working long hours without pause – supported by science and economics – is that, actually, it takes you further away from success, not closer to it.

THE SCOOP

The Hard Work Myth fuels the idea that we can achieve more by working harder, but study the world's top business leaders and you'll see their success has nothing to do longer hours, and everything to do with working smart and respecting what is needed to maximize peak productivity. Realize this, and you're closer to unlocking how to really get ahead.

Proof that thrashing yourself doesn't work

Japan is a nation that has coined a word for death by overwork. Victims of 'karoshi' normally die by committing suicide or suffer heart attacks and strokes.

So extreme, so punishing are some white-collar workplaces that karoshi has been officially recognized and documented by Japan's Ministry of Labour since the late 1980s.

More than a fifth of Japanese workers clock up an average of 49 hours or longer at work each week, compared to 16.4% of workers in the US, 12.5% in Britain and 10.1% in Germany[3].

There's also a Japanese word for napping at work, 'inemuri', which is perceived as a sign of diligence and commitment to work.

And yet, Japan's productivity statistics – based on Gross Domestic Product per hour worked – are languishing at the bottom of the G7.

Further evidence that output does not improve based on increased hours put in, comes from the OECD (2015) which lists productivity and hours worked in 35 countries. It reveals Mexico to be the least productive while also having the world's longest average working week at 41.2 hours. That's no coincidence, and neither is the fact that Luxembourg, the most productive country on that list, has an average working week of just 29 hours[4].

Humans need rest. Unless you have a rare gene mutation that means you can function beautifully on four to six hours' sleep per night – and only 1% of the human race is thought to be blessed with it – then not getting enough sleep can make you less productive by affecting

---

[3]As reported by the Associated Press
[4]See the OECD league table on Time.com

your performance and even accelerate your journey on the road to death.

A study, published in the Journal of Sleep Research, and based on data collected from a cohort of almost 44,000 adults in a lifestyle and medical survey conducted in Sweden in 1997, followed the fate of participants for up to 13 years after. It found that under 65s who got five hours of sleep or less on seven days per week had a 65% higher mortality rate than those getting six or seven hours of sleep[5].

Are no-sleep entrepreneurs really prepared to take premature death as an acceptable loss?

The hidden cost of working harder

When you have a powerful drive to achieve more, pushing yourself harder seems the obvious solution, especially to those of us who have grown up believing The Hard Work Myth.

When faced with a stack of work we simply put in those extra hours to clear the backlog, extending our time at the office or squeezing it into the weekend. We figure it won't always be like this.

Before we know it, that increased workload is no longer the exception, but the new normal.

---

[5]Study published 22 May 2018 on Wiley.com

You can't 'see' or 'count' the cost. It's insidious, slowly creeping up on you – uninvited and totally undetectable – until it's too late.

You don't have to be a scientist to know that the more you work, the less energy you will have.

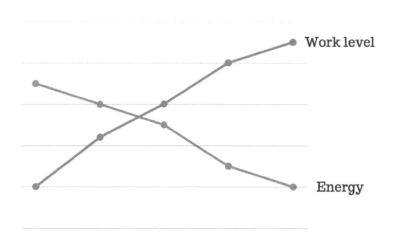

Every time you skip a break, power on late in to the evening, or work weekends, you deplete those finite energy levels. The good news is that your energy is a renewable resource, but workaholics don't give themselves time to fully charge before going for it again.

Do this regularly for long enough, and you're trapped in a vicious circle. All the time, your energy levels get lower and lower, because they have no chance to recover.

Working harder and harder eats away, with an ever-insatiable appetite, at your bottom line by slowly eroding what you can achieve in a day. Eventually, you end up exhausted, mentally, physically and emotionally.

This is known as the law of diminishing returns: there comes a point at which the benefits gained are less than the amount of energy invested. That point is slightly different for everyone.

One study of British civil servants, which looked at the association between long working hours and cognitive function in middle age, found those who worked 55 hours per week scored lower on cognitive tests spanning memory, reasoning and vocabulary compared to those who worked up to a maximum of 40 hours a week[6]. And an Australian study suggests mental health may begin to decline once the 39 hours per week threshold is breached[7].

You might be thinking: "I enjoy hard work! I can style it out. I'll grab a coffee if I'm tired." But let's get to the real cost of thrashing yourself.

The energy you're losing by working harder is the very same energy you need to be using on your strategy, vision and ideas, in order to achieve more.

---

[6]*Long Working Hours and Cognitive Function: The Whitehall II Study* (March 2009)
[7]*Hour-glass ceilings: Work-hour thresholds, gendered health inequities* (March 2017)

In turn, your ability to 'see' where your business is heading, to come up with the ideas, to solve problems and to think about the future reduces and, eventually, disappears.

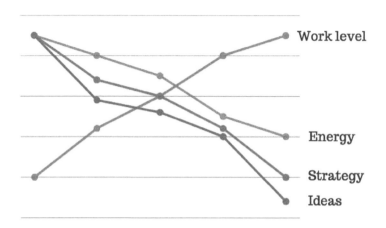

Have you ever felt less able to cope when problems and challenges arise? Have you ever felt deflated because the reality of running your business seems to have got in the way of your original idea? Do you often feel tired and unusually emotional? Chances are, your work and energy are out of balance.

Imagine sprinting while trying to read a map. Doing both is almost impossible because you can't hold the map still enough to read it. The sensible solution is to stop for a moment, catch your breath, look at the map and work out where to go next. But many of us are nevertheless attempting the impossible - to keep running at pace and hope we've picked the right direction.

We all heed the notion of 'quality over quantity' and yet many of us still believe the myth that hard work alone can help us succeed.

In an interview with the president of the Economic Club Washington DC David Rubenstein, Amazon founder Jeff Bezos said: "If I make, like, three good decisions a day, that's enough. And they should be as high quality as I can make them. Warren Buffett says he's good if he makes three good decisions a year."

Here's the exciting thing. Once you realize that by working harder you are directly reducing the energy you need to achieve more, you can start to make some incredibly powerful changes.

When I was working 100 hours a week my business was flatlining. It barely grew for about four years. I was pushing and pushing, working longer and longer hours and nothing seemed to work.

And what happened when I made my change and started working 35-hour weeks? My business started to grow. In the first year after that change, our revenue grew by 275%, we launched in a second continent and we welcomed thousands of new customers.

Over-working is always your choice

When you call the shots in your business, you also call the shots on your time, meaning fatigue and burnout caused by failure to rest, break and refresh are self-inflicted.

Motivated by success or money, or fuelled by the commitment to an idea, entrepreneurs can become obsessive. Many of us allow work to consume our minds, our energy and our time.

You might recognize yourself as a micro-manager, also known as a control freak. You are someone who cannot trust and cannot delegate so you must take on everything yourself, or check your team's work rigorously.

Or perhaps you are an overachiever running from failure. You push yourself harder to postpone the reality that you might fail, and paper over the cracks that suggest you are already failing, instead of using the opportunity to build something that really works.

If you don't recognize yourself in any of these groups, you could be a victim of FOMO (fear of missing out).

You believe that if you step away from the business for a vacation you'll miss the next big new business win.

You think the new client or new project pipeline will stagnate if you're not there to drive it.

Many people who work 100-hour weeks don't realize that it is their choice. It feels like something you *have* to do. *"I would have finished on time but then that email came in"* or *"I don't like to work at the weekends but I had to get that pitch done before Monday".*

How to reduce the hours you work

Ask yourself this simple question: how many hours per week would you like to work? For me, 35 hours seemed like a realistic and sensible goal that would give me the time I wanted with my family.

As soon as I'd set the number of hours I wanted to work, I was forced to make some changes. I started scheduling my time to avoid working late into the night. I stopped checking my email an hour before leaving the office to avoid getting dragged into last-minute issues. And I began planning ahead so that I'd get things ready for next week well ahead of time.

It wasn't hard to implement a few little rules, but the impact was immeasurable.

1. Swap working harder for working on the right stuff

When growing a business or when faced with complex problems, we all work harder by default, because it's easier to do that than it is to be selective about what we're working on.

Being picky about the tasks you're working on takes an enormous amount of thinking time, strategy and discipline so many of us simply avoid it, preferring to soldier on with our to-do lists instead. It's easier to jump straight in and start doing stuff, rather than taking the time to pause and think.

But if you reduce the number of hours you work every day, you're forced to be much more selective over what you work on. You very quickly have to work out what things push your business forward, and commit to only these tasks.

I've covered how to decide what to work on and how to delegate elsewhere in this book, but here is a flavor of what this meant for me:

What sort of things did I delegate?

- Ordering snacks for the office (I kid you not...)
- Filing my emails into folders
- Screening CVs from people who wanted to work for us

What sort of tasks did I keep for myself?

- One-on-one conversations with people on my team
- Thinking about the direction I wanted the business to go in
- Creative control of our website

2. Consider taking a regular 'workcation'

It's our perception that working harder and harder is the way to make money, be successful and get ahead. As we've seen, Japan and Mexico are proof that, in fact, it's doing quite the opposite.

Internal research by EY has found that breaks have a direct and transformative effect on performance. In the U.S. and Canada, the company found that for each 10 vacation hours a person took, performance reviews were, on average 8 per cent higher.[8]

---

[8]As reported on CNBC

Even so, the average U.S. employee only took 16.8 days of their average allowance of 22.6 days in 2016, according to the *Project: Time Off* report[9]. The same report also revealed that self-proclaimed 'work martyrs' are less likely to have had a raise or bonus in the past three years and no more likely to have received a promotion in the past year than those employees who do not subscribe to the work martyrdom.

While these surveys were based on employees rather than entrepreneurs, the findings are still relevant. Clearly, those who sacrifice vacation to 'get ahead' are failing, based on two metrics. The hours put in clearly have no positive impact on success.

I've spoken to hundreds of high achieving entrepreneurs who all have the same complaint. They say that it's impossible to take a vacation, despite their friends and family urging them to.

I had the same problem. Even with my shorter weeks, I found taking vacations tough. Often the backlog of work, issues and communication when I got back would dominate for at least a couple of weeks. It simply didn't feel worth it.

So I invented the 'workcation': every three months, I step away from my business for three or four days to

---

[9]*Project: Time Off* report: ustravel.org/research/state-american-vacation-2018

take stock, celebrate wins, scrutinize losses and plan our move for the next quarter.

This is not a vacation in the traditional sense. It's a working break that gives me the headspace to focus *on* my business, not *in* my business, but with none of the fall-out from going cold turkey and not touching my business, email or phone for a week.

It's a period of reflection and activity, and it always offers perspective. When you see your future in three-month blocks, rather than as an endless stretch of time to retirement, everything suddenly seems easier, and vastly more enjoyable.

Knowing when to walk away from your business takes time to learn. This is not only an administrative change, but it's also a mindset change. It's about seeing breaks as something you *have* to take for the good of your personal health and the good of your business.

CHAPTER TWO

IT STARTS WITH SELF-AWARENESS

"I think self-awareness is probably the most important thing towards being a champion."
– Billie Jean King

One sunny afternoon, I was working through a problem at Time Etc HQ, which is on the 14th-floor of a building overlooking a leafy part of Birmingham, Britain's second largest city. I wanted to figure out how to encourage our newest clients to delegate their very first task to a virtual assistant.

Because the prospect of handing over work can feel daunting, we found new clients were putting off getting started. We also knew that if we could just get them over that first hurdle, they'd be so impressed, they'd send over more work. But how to convince them?

As I mulled this over at my desk, I had a 'hey presto' moment. By adding a simple five-minute countdown timer to the page I could create a sense of urgency.

I turned to our chief operating officer, Kirsten Glaze, who sits next to me, and said: "Can I talk to you for a second?". As I started to open my mouth to tell her about my idea, she interrupted me.

"Stop", she said, "You've just solved something haven't you?". Surprised, I replied: "Well yes, but how on earth did you know that?"

"Because in all the years we've worked together, you've almost always come to me with your best ideas at exactly the same time, just after 4pm. I can almost set my watch by it!"

I was intrigued, was I really that predictable?

The more I thought about it, the more I realized what Kirsten had noticed was true. Curious, I started to pay closer attention to my productivity highs and lows.

The afternoons that produced the most powerful ideas were always preceded by me having cleared my routine tasks in the morning and either dealt with any distractions that had come up early or ignored them altogether. I'd eaten a good, healthy lunch and had a couple of coffees.

In contrast, the low-output days had seen me skip lunch or bolt down something bad, procrastinate on my routine tasks in the morning and allow distractions – like meetings and phone calls – into my afternoon.

It didn't take Sherlock Holmes to figure out that I could have more productive, satisfying and idea-filled work days by simply controlling distractions, avoiding procrastination in the mornings, eating a healthy lunch every day and keeping the afternoons clear of meetings.

And that's exactly what I started doing.

Why am I telling you this story? Time after time, I've found that awareness, just like the awareness that Kirsten triggered in me, is the most fundamental and powerful tool in seeing off The Hard Work Myth and achieving more, without working harder.

Swap your *autopilot* for *awareness* and, like me, you'll be able to optimize your days to get more done and feel at your most productive.

THE SCOOP

Greater self-awareness leads to more work completed in less time. Why? Because your working week can be structured around your personal productivity highs and lows. To beat The Hard Work Myth, pay closer attention to the times of day you work best and worst, and the variable factors that can boost or damage your output.

Many of the world's most successful entrepreneurs are highly self-aware. Just look at Jeff Bezos who – as we saw in the previous chapter – plans his work day around his cognitive abilities, which he knows are impaired by the end of the day due to decision fatigue. He said: "By 5pm I'm like 'I can't think about this today, let's try that again tomorrow at 10am'."

By being incredibly self-aware, and openly embracing his weaknesses, Bezos has smashed The Hard Work Myth. He knows the value he can add to Amazon is in the two or three high-quality decisions he can make each day, before his energy fades. These decisions have helped to make hundreds of billions of dollars for Amazon over the past 25 years.

From the 1980s, Microsoft founder Bill Gates ritually cut himself off from his business, family, friends and colleagues twice a year to take a 'Think Week'. Holed up in a secluded cabin in a forest, Gates mainly used the time to read through hundreds of innovation ideas from employees. He knew this was the best way to commit to the Herculean effort of reading, absorbing and responding to all those papers, by removing all the many distractions – including technology – that threatened his productivity and clamored for his attention every day.

Being self-aware – of your vulnerability to distractions, or the fact you're an utterly useless human being before 10am and a strong espresso – is arguably just as important as being aware of your strengths, but it's something that many of us don't like to share with our employees.

By contrast, many of the world's most successful entrepreneurs are really open about their weaknesses.

Billionaire Sir Richard Branson, who has built hundreds of businesses around the world, recently declared that he hadn't understood the difference between net and gross profit until he was 50-years-old and someone explained the concept to him using a fishing net and some pieces of paper[10].

Branson's self-awareness led him to delegate all financial responsibilities within his empire from the very earliest days, but imagine if he hadn't been so self-aware. If he'd tried to do the numbers in his small Virgin company, would it have grown into the billion-dollar group that it is today with airlines, railways, real estate and hundreds of other investments?

A 2010 study by Green Peak Partners and Cornell's School of Industrial and Labor Relations found a high self-awareness score to be the strongest predictor of overall success[11]. The report added: "This is not altogether surprising as executives who are aware of their weaknesses are often better able to hire subordinates who perform well in categories in which the leader lacks acumen. These leaders are also more able to entertain the idea that someone on their team may have an idea that is even better than their own."

To summarize, knowing yourself well lets you optimize how to work, when to work and what to work on.

---

[10]Read this at
www.virgin.com/richard-branson/how-i-learned-difference-between-net-and-gross
[11]As reported on Forbes

How to develop better self-awareness

The discoveries I've made about myself have not only helped me to achieve more without working harder, they've also contributed more to my personal life than anything else that I've learned, invested in or done in that time.

My relationships have improved, I am less irritable, I feel less stressed and, most of the time, I am able to truly switch off from my work when I get home. I've learned to control my compulsions and even managed to conquer some seriously ingrained habits, built over many years.

As my awareness has increased, so has the revenue and profit in my business. Why? Because I'm able to focus like never before. My self-awareness keeps me laser-focused on the things that directly contribute to our goals as a business. I'm able to detect when we're drifting off focus as a team, and put us back on track.

If you want to achieve more without working harder, and beat The Hard Work Myth, then self-awareness is half the battle. You'll be able to make sure that you're at your desk during the hours when you produce your best work, and in meetings when you feel most able to engage with others. You'll be able to time your breaks when your productivity habitually plummets.

Building your self-awareness is a prerequisite for getting the maximum impact from the rest of this book.

Everything that follows will become easier and more powerful when combined with a healthy level of self-awareness.

I can't give you self-awareness, only you can do that. The great thing is that you can start improving it today. This isn't about meditating or going on retreats to find yourself, this is about noticing and observing small things that repeat.

You might already know some of the following statements to be true about yourself:

- I like to leave my afternoons free to focus on one thing
- I cannot multitask
- I procrastinate if a task is too big or requires a lot of brainpower
- Towards the end of the week, I find it easier to get into a flow
- I can do more in one 1.5-hour slot late in the afternoon than the whole morning
- If I skip lunch, I'll have crashed by 3pm
- If I do some exercise before work, I concentrate better all morning
- If I drink even one glass of wine in the evening, I'll feel groggy until 11am the next day

Some of these are really basic nuggets of self-awareness. Some you'll already know about. But there are many more that you won't have unearthed yet.

Some, you will have been oblivious to for years.

I have used these little bits of self-awareness to create some simple rules I work by:

- I never try to work on two things at once because I cannot multitask
- I break big tasks down into smaller ones to avoid procrastinating
- I book at least one day off once a month that's just for me
- I plan an easy Monday as I'm always tired from the weekend
- I plan all my creative and writing work for Fridays when I find I can focus better

Making these simple changes has had big results.

Having worked long hours for years with hardly anything to show for it, I can almost guarantee that every day is now productive and enjoyable so I can go home feeling satisfied and happy.

Here are some questions you can ask yourself today to begin growing your self-awareness. Jot down the answers to create your own set of rules:

- What environment do you work best in?
- When do you work best?
- At what time of day do you have your best ideas?
- How much sleep do you need?
- Do you prefer lists or schedules?
- Do you work better with the pressure of deadlines or without?
- What excites you about work?
- What angers you about work?
- When do you tend to feel happiest or saddest?
- What has happened on the 'good' days?
- What are you always distracted by?

The answers to these questions will help you map out your perfect working week and working environment.

Self-awareness is a truly powerful thing. It's your fuel for optimizing what you're able to get done in a day, and for creating a routine that suits your energy highs and lows.

And it is fundamental to shattering The Hard Work Myth.

CHAPTER THREE

DEALING WITH DISTRACTIONS

"I think self-awareness is probably the most important thing towards being a champion."
– *Billie Jean King*

I love taking my kids to the circus. Even for a man in his mid-thirties, there is still magic to be found inside that big top tent. But when I was a child, it was a very different experience: live animals were part of the show.

One act – the lion tamer – always fascinated me. While he always carried a whip and a chair into the ring, the whip was never used. How could a vulnerable human control such a huge beast that could maul and kill him at will?

It wasn't until years later that I discovered the answer. In his amusing book, *How Does Aspirin Find A Headache?* author David Feldman explains that, rather than being scared of the whip, the lion is, in fact, distracted by the chair. The lion tries to focus on all four legs at once, and, as a result, is frozen to the spot.

I'd like to put it to you that you are that frozen lion, only, instead of a chair, you're faced with the barrage of daily distractions.

THE SCOOP

Distractions are all around us, all the time. If you want to beat The Hard Work Myth and achieve more without working harder then you must build a defense mechanism against them. This starts with learning to identify the difference between a distraction and a legitimate task for your to-do list.

Distractions threaten our success

How often do you begin the day with great intentions, only to finish it feeling like you never really started what you set out to do? A feeling that you've been busy all day, but somehow lacking the sense of fulfillment you'd hoped for?

Distractions are the culprit: that sales call from an insurance company, that email from your accountant, the news headlines, social media feeds, the customer who needs urgent attention, the car service you urgently need to schedule.

Distractions – some created by work, others a product of life – sneak in, legitimized by us as things we absolutely *have to do* at this very moment. We allow them to take number one priority without question.

Humans enjoy distractions, which explains why we're always trying to find them. Why? They spare us from the really difficult tasks we need to devote time to and exhaust brain power on. They rescue us from having to face the reality of figuring out how to solve complex problems.

And some distractions – like planning that dream vacation to wine country – can even be downright enjoyable.

We feel good about being able to complete a simple task like answering an email. Sure, it's distracting us from the bigger task at hand, but at least you've done something. Right? WRONG!

That little endorphin hit – that lovely buzz we get from finishing a task – is addictive. If you replace your big goal for the day with smaller distractions, even if each one only takes 10 minutes to finish, it pushes you further away from that goal and from achieving more.

A study by researchers at the University of California, Irvine, found the typical office worker is interrupted, or switches tasks, every three minutes and five seconds. And, after an interruption, it can take just over 23 minutes to refocus and get back to the original task at hand[12]. Suddenly, it becomes clear how easy it is to lose a whole working day to dealing with distractions.

Reacting to distractions means that you're giving your mind, at once, to anyone and anything. Every time you're distracted, you're diverting time, energy and focus away from work that makes you achieve more and replacing it with work that simply fills a time void. It's a really bad value exchange.

Distractions steal your time and elongate your working day. But eliminate them, and you will have done The Hard Work Myth some serious damage.

Technology: the new distraction threat

Distractions aren't a new problem. According to Jamie Kreiner, associate professor of history at the University of Georgia, medieval monks had a big problem with distraction: they complained about information overload, being distracted by staring out of the window, and

---

[12]Results of the study are at www.ics.uci.edu/~gmark/chi08-mark.pdf

finding themselves thinking about food or sex when they were supposed to be thinking about God[13].

Ancient Buddhists coined the term Vikṣepa, which can be translated as 'distraction' or 'mental wandering'. Along with laziness and inattentiveness, it was believed to be one of the 20 destabilizing factors of the mind.

Today, when it comes to eliminating distractions, we have a distinct disadvantage over the medieval monks and ancient Buddhists: technology.

We all live in a permanent state of distraction. With smartphones at our fingertips, we no longer have any reason to be bored. The result is that we've forgotten how to focus.

How often does your hand reach for your phone without the conscious mind telling it to? How much time passes as you scroll through feeds on Instagram, Facebook, and Twitter, or watching videos on YouTube?

Americans spend more than four hours a day on their phones[14]. The average person checks their cell 47 times per day; 89% do so within an hour of waking up and 81% within an hour of going to sleep[15].

---

[13]As summarised at
aeon.co/ideas/how-to-reduce-digital-distractions-advice-from-medieval-monks
[14]As referenced on FT.com
[15]According to Deloitte's 2018 global mobile consumer survey: US edition

The feeling of boredom now triggers an habitual action: we reach for our smartphones to connect with others, or to find a podcast, game, e-book or article that passes the time.

We've all formed now-ingrained habits, prompted by clever notifications designed to elicit responses, like that little dopamine hit from receiving likes and messages that keeps you craving more. In short, our smartphone apps have been engineered by software designers to be addictive and distracting.

Ex-Facebook President Sean Parker made a then-startling announcement while speaking at an event in 2017 when he said the social media site was built to exploit "a vulnerability in human psychology" using a "social-validation feedback loop"[16].

Parker admitted that Facebook "probably interferes with your productivity in weird ways" and said the team who launched the social media platform was trying to figure out from the start how to "consume as much of your time and conscious attention as possible".

This idea was given further fuel by ex-Googler Tristan Harris in his TED Talk: *How a handful of tech companies control billions of minds every day*[17]. In it, he talks about how global dotcoms are in a "race for our

---

[16]Watch the interview in full on the Axios website
[17]It's 17 minutes long and well worth a watch on Ted.com

attention" and competing over who can "go lower" to get it. He believes humans must acknowledge they are "persuadable" if we are to move forward with technology in a healthy and positive way.

This wasn't the way it was supposed to go. You bought your smartphone to make your working and personal life easier to manage on the go. If it makes you unhappy, keeps you awake at night, distracts you, or helps you to procrastinate, then it's not doing its job.

Thrive Global and HuffPost founder Ariana Huffington wrote: "Technology is granting us unprecedented power and opportunities to do amazing things - but it's also accelerated the pace of our lives beyond our capacity to keep up. We all feel it - we're being controlled by something we should be controlling... This – our relationship with technology – is what's going to be the protagonist of the next ten years of this story."[18]

How to beat distractions

Some of the world's most successful entrepreneurs have created techniques for dealing with emails which, though unavoidable, are also widely regarded as one of the biggest distractions to work productivity.

---

[18]For more on Huffington's struggle with burnout, visit https://bit.ly/2OQID6W

Like many business owners, LinkedIn CEO Jeff Weiner relies heavily on email, and describes his inbox as "the central hub of [his] workflow." But, he has learned to send fewer emails so that he receives fewer emails[19]. His realization came after two people he worked closely with, who were "highly effective communicators", left the company and his inbox traffic reduced by 20-30%.

Similarly, Zappos CEO Tony Hsieh, after finding that it was virtually impossible to reach "inbox zero" started an email management technique he dubbed 'Yesterbox'[20]. In short, he deals with yesterday's emails today. This way, he knows exactly how many emails he has to deal with, and there's a satisfying sense of completion once the job is done.

A simple five-step process for dealing with distractions

It's time to realize that dealing with constant distractions – however fast and efficiently you can rattle through them – is false productivity.

Distractions are masterful at preventing you from achieving growth. They are ultimately doing a brilliant job at keeping your business small. But you have the

---

[19]Published on LinkedIn in a piece titled 7 Ways to Manage Email So It Doesn't Manage You
[20]There is even a dedicated Yesterbox website

power to stop them. Here is the five-step process I use for identifying and handling distractions.

By adopting this system, you can dramatically reduce the frequency, volume and impact of distractions on your productivity and, as a result, be intensely focused during the very limited hours you plan to work.

1. Identify them

First, realize and accept how distracted we all are. If we can identify and be conscious of distractions, we can start building a defense against them.

This is easier said than done. It's easy to realize after dealing with something that it was a distraction, but much more difficult in the moment.

Train yourself to pause after you've received an email, or a colleague stops to speak to you. Simply pausing, momentarily, to ask the question: "Is this a distraction?" can be a very powerful change.

2. Make a list

Compiling a list of your top distractions will help you build awareness so you can begin to shut them down as they arise.

The key here is to identify the enemy because, once we know what we're likely to be distracted by, it's so much easier to prevent it from taking our time.

I bet my list of distractions looks a lot like yours:

- My phone
- Responding to emails
- Meetings
- Requests for help from my team
- Social media feeds and notifications

If you're struggling to come up with a list of distractions, you can flip this around and do it another way by compiling a daily shortlist of the goals you need to achieve by close of business. Anything not on that list is a distraction to be avoided.

3. Challenge every distraction

When a distraction on your list next arises, ask yourself this question: "Will doing this task now directly help me achieve my goals?" If the answer is no, then don't take any action. If the answer is yes, then ask yourself: "Exactly how will this help me reach my goals?"

A word of warning here. The number one issue with distractions is that we legitimize them. We say: "I need to get back to this client otherwise they'll take their business elsewhere and if they do that my revenue will drop which means I won't reach my revenue target." This might feel very plausible, but it's your mind maneuvering to justify the distraction. Will the client *really* go elsewhere if they don't get a reply instantly? What's the likelihood of them actually leaving?

A leap of faith may be required here. When you first stop immediately acting on distractions, especially ones that seem of critical importance, it can feel like a step backward. Many of us pride ourselves on our rapid responses or attentive service.

But very rarely does not reacting immediately cause the other person to question our service to them. In fact, over time, people get used to your typical response time.

If you're really concerned, add a note to your email signature, such as: "So I can work effectively, I usually only deal with my inbox between 4pm and 5pm, so please forgive any short delays in my response time."

We also need to look at the much bigger picture here. As you grow and develop as an entrepreneur, freelancer or leader, you need to find new ways of working that aren't just reactive and distraction led. By learning how to manage distractions and prevent them from getting in the way, you're proactively giving yourself the space to grow your leadership, talent and service to others, which benefits everyone.

4. If they can't disappear, store them up for later

I estimate that 70% of the distractions that interrupt my day can be safely left without me needing to take any action. These distractions simply disappear in time.

For me, these tend to be cold sales approaches by email, LinkedIn requests from people I don't know, voicemails from service providers who want to check in with me or upsell to me and so on.

The other 30% of distractions won't just disappear, however, and need to be dealt with. Your brain may trick you into thinking these distractions are urgent, so how can we stop them stealing your time and focus?

The answer is to write them down and then schedule a strictly limited time slot in your day to perform a 'Distraction Demolition'. This is an intensive period in which you deal with everything that has made the distraction list in one fell swoop.

I schedule my Distraction Demolition for an hour every other morning. In that hour I'll quickly blitz my list, firing off emails in response, taking actions and resolving things. When the hour is up, I move on to my day's work, leaving anything I didn't get to for next time.

By compressing your distractions into a limited time period you win back control of your time and focus.

5. Delegate repeating distractions

Chances are, once you start looking in detail at your distractions you'll notice that some occur time and again, daily, weekly or monthly.

If these distractions can't be prevented, you should delegate them to someone who can handle them on your behalf, such as an assistant or member of your team, or look to automate them.

Business expenses, booking travel tickets, and setting up meetings are all things that can be delegated, leaving you distraction-free.

If you're not in the habit, passing over tasks can take some getting used to, but if you start with distractions you're guaranteed to feel an instant benefit.

And delegating handling distractions that recur is a double win: not only will you be free from something that repeatedly steals your focus but, more than likely, you'll only have to delegate it once, saving you potentially hundreds of hours over the next few years with a small investment of your time.

We'll take a closer look at this in the chapter *Deconstructing Delegation.*

CHAPTER FOUR

TIME FOR A HEALTHY INFORMATION DIET

"Getting information off the internet is like taking a drink from a fire hydrant."
– Mitch Kapor

On a frosty morning in January 2015 I was working from my home office. My house was freezing, so I made myself a large cup of coffee, sunk into my big leather armchair and started browsing the MailOnline.

Reading this opinionated U.K. tabloid was, at the time, a habit of mine, that continued throughout the day.

As I scrolled down the homepage on that particular day, I noticed a headline about a Jordanian pilot who'd been captured and tortured by terrorists. Without really thinking about it, I clicked the link. To this day, I wish I hadn't.

What I saw on that page was an auto-playing video showing the very public and barbaric murder of Muath Safi Yousef al-Kasasbeh, who was burned to death.

As soon as I realized what I was watching, I felt sick. I was in shock, faced with the horror and sadness of seeing a fellow human murdered in front of my eyes as he frantically tried to escape.

That experience had a profound effect on me. Something changed. Over the coming weeks, concerned by how simply reading the news could cause such intense fear and anxiety, I started to unpick the content machine and became far more protective over what I would consume. As I did so, I started to notice a positive impact on my life and my work.

Content, content, everywhere

News, social media platforms and websites feed us articles, videos, podcasts, opinions, ideas, comments, photos and data of varying quality, every minute of every day.

Much of what we consume is in a state of partial sleep, unconsciously picking up our smartphones without being fully aware of what we're doing. If we were more aware, we might notice that much of the content we consume is distracting, boring, plagiarized and possibly even fake.

News has never stopped, and now we need never stop reading it. This feeds The Hard Work Myth, because the distractions that have the power to change our moods and emotions are the most threatening of all. If you're thrown off course by a harrowing story, it's very difficult to cast it out of your mind and refocus. The result is that we end up working harder to compensate for the time lost.

Three major problems with today's online content

1. Headlines are deliberately alluring, but the content is often poor

Headlines are written to hook you. So-called 'clickbait' is used by reliable media outlets, as well as more unscrupulous media companies, to convert you from a feed browser to a page reader, because if you don't click, the publishers don't make any money.

Now, more than ever, the news we consume provides little or no value. Ever tapped on a headline that warns of extreme weather events heading in your direction, only to find the article says nothing of the sort?

There's a reason for this. Weather stories are among the biggest drivers of traffic to news websites. These sites aren't producing content because it's in the public interest, they're producing content that gets people in front of ads.

Google a "how-to" on almost any subject and you'll discover the first few pages of search results are packed with generic and low-value articles that don't really give you the answer you're looking for.

Why don't these articles help? Many are not written by experts but by search engine optimization (SEO) experts working for brands and companies who use a series of cleverly constructed keywords and phrases to make sure you land on their content first.

These articles are designed for one thing: to get your click.

How many times have you clicked on a headline in your Facebook feed and been disappointed by what appears? How often have you felt misled by the promise of the headline? How many times have you idly browsed your 'news' feed on LinkedIn and thought, well that's 15 minutes of my life I'll never get back?

2. We are hooked on sites that deliver garbage

The apps and social platforms we use every day have been engineered by developers to get us hooked. The aforementioned MailOnline – one of the biggest news sites in the world with more than 180 million monthly unique browsers at the time of writing – has a column of thumbnail pictures down the right-hand side of its homepage that has been dubbed 'the sidebar of shame'.

It is notoriously difficult to stop clicking on despite offering lowbrow, gossip-fuelled articles.

Striking a healthier balance with technology has little to do with willpower. We're fighting multi-billion-dollar technology companies who are manipulating the human brain for their bottom lines.

Worth adding to your reading list is behavioral psychologist Nir Eyal's book *Hooked: How to Build Habit-Forming Products*. In it, he explains how we have become attached to social media and the cunning ways tech giants get us addicted to their products.

In short, he explains how user behavior is engineered by guiding us through a series of the same 'hooks' time and again. This makes us form habits, at which point external triggers like push notifications are no longer needed because they have been replaced by internal triggers. Essentially, we become hardwired to associate social media content and reactions with serving our own emotional needs and we pick up our phones to get that fix.

Ever noticed that you spend more time on social media when you find yourself bored, procrastinating or when you're feeling stressed? This suggests you have learned to associate content on your social media feed with preferable emotions. You are hooked.

This, explains Eyal, allows companies to bring users back repeatedly, saving money on costly marketing and advertising.

4. Most 'real' news is really sad

There's a good reason news stations finish a broadcast with stories about skateboarding cats or pug fashion shows. And there's a reason you occasionally find yourself watching home video edits of babies laughing hysterically, or sloths being massaged. It's because news today is so rarely positive.

We, as a society, are desperate for escapism from the reports on crime, political upheaval, injustice and chaos, the environmental crisis, frequently delivered with a dose of drama and hyperbole by subjective news anchors. It's enough to turn even the most optimistic person into a quivering heap.

A survey by the American Psychological Association found that people feel conflicted between their desire to stay informed and their view of the media as a source of stress[21]. It found that while 95% of adults follow the news regularly, 56% say doing so causes them stress, and 72% believe the media blows things out of proportion. But 9% check the news at least every hour and 20% look at social media constantly.

THE SCOOP

The content we see every day has great power over us. It can affect our mood, throw our focus, and dominate our thoughts as we ruminate over what we've just read, or share articles with friends in an effort to make sense of them. Given its irrelevance over what we do at work – and the fact that it's simply not conducive to productivity – this kind of distraction should be far more unwelcome. Adjusting how we consume content is, therefore, key to busting The Hard Work Myth.

---

[21]See the APA survey here: https://bit.ly/2MeBDxT

High achievers read differently

I'm not saying don't read. Most successful people read heavily. But being able to do that requires sacrificing the unnecessary, by which I mean articles written for content marketing purposes, the never-ending stream of public opinion on social media, and up-to-the-minute rolling news that has little bearing over how you make a living.

Successful people don't read to be entertained – that's a bonus – they read to nourish themselves, to deepen their knowledge and to be educated.

Microsoft mogul Bill Gates famously finds the time to devour 50 books a year, and Berkshire Hathaway chairman and CEO Warren Buffett credits reading as the key to his business success. He gets through 500 pages a day – sometimes double that in the early years of his investing career – and he devotes an incredible 80% of his day to reading.

Self-made billionaire Oprah Winfrey started reading at three years old. She started Oprah's Book Club in 1996 and distributes free books to member libraries all over the US. She credits her success with the education she received from reading books, and has said they "set her free".

What you read is just as important as how much. In his book *Rich Habits: The Daily Success Habits of Wealthy Individuals*, Tom Corley contrasts the reading habits of the rich and the poor.

He defines the rich as having an annual income of $160,000+ and a liquid net worth of $3.2million+, while the poor are classed as having an annual income of $35,000 or less and a liquid net worth of $5,000 or less.

He found 79% of poor people read for entertainment, compared to just 11% of rich people, and 85% of rich people read two or more education, career-related or self-improvement books every month, compared to just 15% of poor people[22].

When you're busy, reading two or more books a month is no easy feat; I used to struggle to even read one every six months. But successful, time-poor people are prioritizing their education and self-development through reading, while carefully curating what content they consume, because information makes them more successful.

---

[22]For a summary of Corley's book see https://bit.ly/2qfPOKF

We must defend ourselves from the 'infobesity' epidemic

Bestselling author Sam Horn – a mentor and friend of mine – uses the brilliant term 'infobesity' to describe, in a single word, the deluge of information that threatens to drown us mentally, all day, every day.

Our human brains have a finite capacity for new information. They were never designed to cope with the rapid and non-stop influx of information that we're expected to digest every day.

Behavioral neuroscientist and psychologist Daniel Levitin, who wrote the book: *The Organized Mind: Thinking Straight in the Age of Information Overload*, said: "Our brains are equipped to deal with the world the way it was many thousands of years ago when we were hunter-gatherers... Back then the amount of information that was coming at us was much less and it came at us much more slowly."

If you want to achieve more amid this infobesity epidemic you must put yourself on a strict information diet, refining what goes into your head in order to be more productive, and more successful.

It works like this: when we consume a low-value piece of content there is a consequence. We have less time, less attention and less energy to read, process and store a high-value piece of content - one that could help us achieve more or push our business forward.

You need to be swapping the poor-quality content for powerful content that sparks ideas and helps you achieve more.

How to design the perfect information diet

A healthy information diet can do wonderful things for your entrepreneurial progress and state of mind. You'll find it easy to stick to because, unlike other diets, you're not having to give up the stuff you really enjoy consuming.

With this diet, you're prioritizing the tastiest, juiciest and most rewarding information and throwing away the garbage that leaves you ruminating, feeling bad or simply wastes your time.

1. Create a list of reading material that takes you closer to your goals

Research what you want to know more about. Look for books, audiobooks, and podcasts with advice and learnings from proven experts that might improve and develop you.

To find out how to develop your own reading list, let's go back to Warren Buffett and his business partner at Berkshire Hathaway, Charlie Munger, an equally voracious reader. What are they reading so fervently, and what do they do with the information they absorb?

Speaking to author Michael D. Eisner for his book *Working Together: Why Great Partnerships Succeed,* Buffett said: "We don't read other people's opinions. We want to get the facts, and then think."

Munger once said: "We read a lot. I don't know anyone who's wise who doesn't read a lot. But that's not enough: You have to have a temperament to grab ideas and do sensible things. Most people don't grab the right ideas or don't know what to do with them."

Carefully curated reading, then, needs to become a part of your work goals. By skimming off the fat – junk content that distracts – and replacing it with quality reading material that educates you and deepens your experience, you will have the time for it.

Actioning the ideas you reap from your new and improved reading experience is part and parcel of being a successful business leader, or finding success in your chosen career.

See books as minefields for ideas and their authors as your business mentors. Make time to read and make time to see connections between what you're reading and the next steps to take in your business or career. By putting yourself on a strict information diet you'll be sure you're reading with intent, not reading to procrastinate.

Reading books might be the most valuable thing you do this year for your self-development – because of the value they can add to your life and career – as well as to improve your concentration.

If you're dyslexic and find reading a struggle, learning to give your whole attention and full concentration to an audiobook or podcast could be your goal.

My major goals are to turn my company into a $100M business, enable each member of my team to grow individually and to maintain one of the best company cultures out there, so my reading list is curated to include texts that'll help me reach those goals.

A snapshot of my current reading list:

- *Multipliers* by Liz Wiseman
- *Pig Wrestling* by Pete Lindsay
- *Influence* by Robert Cialdini
- *Dare to Lead* by Brene Brown
- *Delivering Happiness* by Tony Hsieh

2. Cull news and social media from your day

News and social media organizations are very clever. They know they need to manufacture either fear or intrigue to drive traffic.

In his book, *News: A User's Manual*, philosopher Alain de Botton says: "Always remember that the news is always trying to make you scared. It's bad for us, but very good for news organizations: the easiest way to get an audience is through frightening people."

Keeping yourself informed about what's going on in the world, your industry, and the decisions influencing and affecting how you run your business is obviously important. But know this: if something truly important happens, I promise that you will hear about it.

3. Use that time to consume high-quality content

Now that you've identified what content you'd like to consume to help you achieve your goals, you're ready to do the swap.

An easy hack to encourage good reading habits is to have your preferred, quality reading material within easy reach at all times. But replacing the time you'd have spent consuming low-value news and social media content with high-value content isn't a straightforward swap.

Often, low-value content bombards us and distracts throughout our working day, every time we pick up our smartphones. To avoid this you have to create new habits. Start by making a tiny behavior change when you pick up your smartphone - freeze news and social media apps (or better still, remove them completely), and open Kindle or Audible instead.

If you want to make your content consumption even more of a priority, block out time for the high-value stuff by scheduling time in the day to read or listen.

This should be a pleasurable exercise, so make it an event. Move away from your desk, find a comfortable chair in a quiet place, and get a really good cup of coffee. Give yourself an hour.

Alternatively, make better use of your commute, by only reading what's on your list. This can transform dead time into personal development time, twice a day, every day.

CHAPTER FIVE

FEAR AS A FORCE FOR GOOD

"The beautiful thing about fear is, when you run to it, it runs away."
– *Robin Sharma*

A few years ago, I got invited to apply to give a TEDx talk. These smaller independent events mimic the format of TED which began in 1984 and has secured some incredible speakers, from Bill Clinton to Bono.

At the time, public speaking was one of my greatest fears. The notion of standing up in front of a room full of people was, to me, repulsive. I had successfully avoided hundreds of public speaking opportunities over the years, but this one felt different.

I would have been mad to throw away such a great opportunity for exposure so I threw my hat into the ring, and proposed a talk on why breaking the rules is good for you. At this point, I didn't feel scared because I had convinced myself that no one would be interested in what I had to say.

TEDx came back and told me I'd made it through to round two. This was when fear and panic began to kick in. What if I actually had to do this? I forced those familiar, gut-twisting sensations away and filled out the second part of the application.

The organizers came back and accepted my proposal with a list of rules. I was to speak for 15-20 minutes without notes in front of an audience of 200 people. My story had to engage and inspire. I felt like someone had punched me in the stomach.

When I sat down to try and write my speech I found I couldn't form any words because the fear of delivering it was already paralyzing me. The thought of what might go wrong on stage in front of a couple of hundred people was terrifying.

My stomach was already churning and I wasn't even anywhere near a stage. I realized then that I needed to find a way to leave the fear right there and move forward without it or I'd never get my talk written let alone deliver it. So I faced it. I felt my fear and I accepted it.

That simple mindset change meant that, in the coming weeks, I wrote several drafts, memorized the final speech and then practised as though my life depended on it. Turns out, I was the only person who turned up to the rehearsal ready to speak without notes.

I delivered a strong talk I can proudly watch back on YouTube[23]. I was given top billing and opened the whole event. I felt strangely comfortable on stage and I have the fear to thank for that because it gave me the energy to get it right. I learned you can cheat fear by confronting and accepting it, and by not trying to suppress it.

It wasn't a perfect performance; I forgot what I was saying halfway through, but you can't tell because instead of getting upset about it, my brain solved the problem and sewed it all back together.

One speaker on the billing for that same day was terrified. She had to stop 10 or 15 times in her live talk because she was absolutely paralyzed by fear. I could have been in exactly the same boat if I hadn't addressed my fear early on.

Why am I telling you this? Because to achieve more without working harder, you have to function like a well-oiled machine. There is no time for fear, which paralyzes you, cripples you, and slows you down while you ruminate. Learn to harness fear, though, and it can push you closer to your goals. Doing that TEDx talk, for

---

[23]If you have a burning desire to watch a man overcome his greatest fear, watch my Tedx talk here: https://bit.ly/2sXZCJZ

example, put us on the map, helped position me as an authoritative leader and has been viewed by thousands, including many of the people who decided to join our team.

THE SCOOP

Fear can do two things: cripple us or fuel us. The Hard Work Myth is dependent on the former. When you're too scared to act, your business stands still, as you distract yourself with easier, less complex tasks in an effort to feel fulfilled. To beat the myth, learn how to live with fear.

Forge a new, healthy relationship with fear

We're all familiar with fear's myriad manifestations. Often an aching or twisting sensation in the pit of the stomach, coupled with the sweats or shivers and a painfully clenched jaw. The heart beats faster and breathing becomes shallow. The bathroom calls. Rational thoughts abandon ship and the mind goes horribly blank.

If you trace it right back, fear is a primal instinct. That adrenaline rush is designed to keep us alive when confronted by the risk of injury or death.

Today, this fear-response mode is not required because we're not running from lions or tigers or bears. These symptoms are more likely to precede a public speaking event than a near-death experience – unless you're into base jumping – but they are still concerned with keeping us safe by making us choose between fight or flight.

While it's easy to recognize fear once we're in the grip of it and it's smacking us around the face, many business leaders fail to realize – or will not admit – that fear is stopping them from making a big gutsy move that could shoot them to the next level.

Perhaps because we're grown-ups with dependents, or perhaps because people look to us for leadership and life security in the form of a monthly paycheck, many of us don't want to admit that, actually, we're terrified of making a change or a decision that could have big bad consequences.

The symptoms of fear are so blinding, so overwhelming, that it massively clouds reality and upsets our core belief system. Think back to when you quit that job you didn't love, or before you started your business, and remember how fearful you felt. Everything felt risky and less possible, didn't it? Now, with hindsight, do you still feel such strong fear?

There is a way to change your relationship with fear and to win back control. And win it you must, because the alternative is months or years of stagnation. Without taking planned, strategic risks you cannot expect to grow or achieve more.

I'm not suggesting that you remove fear from your life (it's impossible) or deny it's there - but simply get a little better at recognizing when you're feeling it and how it's impacting your judgments.

Recognizing, understanding and accepting fear is a powerful way to unlock fantastic decisions, strategy and action in your business and will help you achieve more, without working harder.

The fear of fear can be just as crippling

Being scared of public speaking is an interesting fear to consider. What are we actually scared of? There's a primal argument that speaking up in a group scenario puts you at risk of being outcast by your pack, or rejected socially and therefore left vulnerable to attack, but that explanation didn't seem right to me.

My subject matter wasn't particularly alienating or controversial. I wasn't particularly scared of being judged because I didn't know the audience personally and I'd probably never see them again.

No, I was scared of those horrible, blinding symptoms of fear; I was scared that they might stop me from delivering my speech, and make me run off stage, or freeze. I feared fear itself.

Virgin boss Sir Richard Branson said: "A touch of the jitters sharpens the mind, gets the adrenaline flowing and helps you focus. It is important not to fear fear, but to harness it — use it as fuel to take your business to the next level. After all, fear is energy."[24]

Branson is right. The adrenaline rush we get when we experience fear is designed to give us superhuman speed to run away, or the strength to fight. It allows us to focus better on the scenario that's presented to us.

Have you ever considered that adrenaline junkies always experience fear in a controlled environment? They are fully prepared for that experience, either because they have trained for years for one particular moment, or because they trust their gear and equipment and ability.

When a person decides to jump off a bridge tethered to a bungee cord, the conscious mind reasons the scenario is safe, allowing that person to feel the fear,

---

[24]From a guest post in Forbes

know they won't die, laugh afterwards with the relief they indeed survived, and then move on.

Entrepreneurs, then, need to channel adrenaline junkies. Because entrepreneurs are scared, all the time. But if you push the fear away, it becomes scarier. Feel the fear, prepare well to mitigate the risks, then acknowledge that you are safe because of your preparation.

Fear leads to bad decisions

Fear not only holds us back from taking the plunge and leaping into new projects and ventures but it can also severely impact our decision making.

Studies have found that when fearful people make decisions they are more likely to consider the future to be pessimistic[25]. Fear also introduces a sense of low certainty and a low sense of control into those making decisions. In short, it seriously clouds and changes our judgment.

How does this impact our decision making in real life? Let's say your very best employee comes to you and says they need a change of role. They say they love working with you but desperately need a change of pace. They say they're not sure whether that'll be within

---

[25]Source: _Emotion and Decision Making_ (June 2014)

your business or whether they need to leave and look elsewhere. This is a sensitive and tough situation for anyone to be in, but let's look at how looking at this situation through a lens of fear changes things.

Because you're likely to see a pessimistic outcome when you feel fear, you might believe that the employee secretly wants to go and work elsewhere and that there's no point in trying to accommodate them in your business by changing their role. Because of fear, you might believe that even if you find them a new role they'll go anyway. And fear will also tell you that, whatever you do, the outcome is uncertain.

Take fear away and you might see this situation as an opportunity to take your very best employee and put them in a more productive position in your business. You might see the fact that they came to you first, rather than just leaving, as a huge advantage and be excited to play with their role until they feel the change of pace they crave. You might see their loyalty to you and reward it, to everyone's advantage, by creating a fantastic new role for them.

By being aware of your fear and treating it differently you'll make better decisions, and better decisions mean less wasted time working on the wrong things.

Use fear as energy

The great news is that you can directly convert your fear from a paralyzing feeling into useful energy. You can develop a technique for harnessing the fears you feel to bring good to your business and help you achieve more, rather than letting them consume you, cause stress or harm your business.

Here's how to do it:

1. Feel the fear, recognize it's there
2. Confront it: write down the cause of the fear
3. Consider your two options: what will happen if you do react to the fear and if you don't
4. Choose one option immediately
5. Leave the fear behind you

Let's look at a real-life example of how fear can get in the way of achieving more if you don't take control of it. Say you've got an unhappy customer in your business. That's a pretty fear-filled situation for most of us. What if they ask for their money back? What if they write a negative review online and harm our reputation? What if I can't make them happy?

If you're not aware of it, the fear wrapped up in all of these questions can dictate how you respond to your unhappy customer and, at worse, completely paralyze you, forcing you to avoid dealing with the unhappy customer altogether.

So how can we use fear in this situation?

1. Feel the fear

Perhaps it kicks in when you open an email from your unhappy customer.

2. Confront it

"I'm feeling fear because I'm worried this customer is going to leave and perhaps even ask for a refund. If they do, they might also write a negative review online which could harm our reputation."

3. Consider your options

Those might be:
- "If I *don't* react to this fear, I'll think clearly and carefully about what would help make this customer happy again."
- Or "If I react to this fear, I might never get back to this customer because I don't know what to say."
- Or "If I react to this fear, I might assume the worst and miss a chance to put things right for this customer."

4. Choose one option immediately

The best option is clearly the first as it's both proactive and positive, and offers the highest chance of rescuing the situation. It could even turn a disgruntled customer into a happy one.

5. Let the fear go

Now that you've chosen an option, you no longer need the fear, and you can safely let it go. Go for a walk, have a breather, move on and release the fear. You've dealt with it!

If you struggle with this, I find something helpful that a friend of mine once suggested, which is to 'jetlag' your fear. In short, you deal with the problem you're facing, and choose to delay confronting the fear until later. By then, more often than not, the fear has simply disappeared.

Changing how you deal with fear, by getting better at recognizing its presence and observing to how you normally respond to it, can directly help you achieve more.

By carefully managing it, you can turn fear from something that can get in the way of you performing at your best and achieving more into a force for good and a positive energy that can be harnessed - helping you make faster, clearer decisions.

CHAPTER SIX

FAILURE BY FREEDOM

"My favorite things in life don't cost any money. It's really clear that the most precious resource we all have is time."
– Steve Jobs

I will never forget the moment I first experienced true freedom. I was five years old and I ran across our little garden, pushed through the old gate at the end and ran into the small field beyond. As I got to the middle of the field, I stopped, took a huge breath and looked up. A bird was soaring high above me, silhouetted against the bright blue sky, and I was awestruck. In that very moment, I understood exactly what freedom felt like.

Fast forward 13 years and I'm coming to the end of high school. My parents are desperate for me to continue with my education and get a university degree, following in the footsteps of my older brother and sister who are well on their way to becoming doctors. But I keep thinking about that day in the field. I want to feel it again, that sense of complete freedom, like anything is possible.

Like many people craving freedom, I don't follow my friends to university or pursue the path my parents want me to take. Instead, I start my own business. Life feels good. There is no one telling me what to do, no rules, and no routine.

Things start to move quickly. My company quickly challenges the established businesses in the market who have long been overcharging people and it's doing well, generating profits. I have no time to stop and think about what I'm doing.

But after two years of growth, my drive begins to stall and my productivity nosedives. I begin each day with good intentions but never quite get to strike off the big-ticket item on my to-do list: there are just too many small jobs to do.

Each day ends with me feeling despondent and irritated. There aren't enough hours in the day and my goals always seem out of reach.

Eventually, the days start blurring into one another until I'm living one long day that spans several months.

I start to procrastinate chronically, so much so I probably get less done in a week than one person on my team gets done in a day.

Hindsight is a wonderful thing. In my bid for total freedom, I had taken my new entrepreneurial lifestyle to the extreme and totally overlooked the very human need for structure, direction and accountability to function, let alone to perform.

The inconvenient truth about entrepreneurial freedom is this: we all love working when we want, deciding what we work on and reporting to absolutely no-one, but these very same benefits can kill our dreams completely.

To beat The Hard Work Myth and achieve more without working harder, you need to take a long, hard look at the freedom you have and consider, is it really serving me?

THE SCOOP

Many of us become entrepreneurs because we crave freedom and power over our time, but a work life without boundaries can be really damaging to our productivity. To compensate, we force ourselves to stay longer at our desks until we've produced something fruitful. Then we beat ourselves up when we give up, tired and frustrated. Freedom is a poisoned chalice. To beat the Hard Work Myth, set your own parameters.

Freedom is rarely what we hope it will be

There is a good reason that millions of skilled, experienced people all over the world choose to work for organizations as employees, rather than for themselves.

The structure, direction, and hierarchy keep people on-track, motivated and productive. Remove these things and most people struggle.

Flexible and agile working is in huge demand in modern workplaces. But, make no mistake, even in companies where employees appear to be granted complete creative freedom, total autonomy, and the ability to work from wherever and whenever they like, boundaries still exist in abundance.

Retail giant Zappos – now owned by Amazon – is famous for its authentic culture and exceptional customer service. Since early 2014, it has operated as a Holacracy, a self-management practice for running purpose-driven companies, created and trademarked by software developer Brian Robertson[26].

Partly designed to stop employees feeling the need to seek approval from management for every small decision and causing gridlock, decisions are made locally by teams. The flat organizational structure is regularly tweaked with small iterations and each team is responsible for organizing itself.

It offers empowerment and autonomy but the whole system is well managed and well structured. In short, the structure enables the freedom.

As Zappos CEO Tony Hsieh explains: "In Holacracy, one of the principles is to make the implicit explicit – tons of it is about creating clarity: who is in charge of what, who is taking what kind of decision – and there is also a system for defining that, and changing that, so it's very flexible at the same time."

---

[26]For more on this see the Holacracy website

At Time Etc, we experimented with offering unlimited flexible working and were surprised that people struggled with it. It demotivated our team and made them uncomfortable. Next, we gave our team the option to work flexibly for three days per month. This has proved far more popular - but why did putting a limit on flexible working get better results?

The workforce today craves flexibility. That's the message employers are getting loud and clear. But the pendulum can swing too far.

Academic research found that empowering workers can cause uncertainty and resentment, while freedom to make their own decisions and work without monitoring can be detrimental to productivity[27].

Total freedom is a poisoned chalice. To be productive and engaged, people need to know what they're doing, and why they're doing it. And the same goes for entrepreneurs, too.

Think back to when you last worked for someone else. I'd put money on these statements being true:

---

[27]More details of the 2017 study by University of Exeter Business School, Alliance Manchester Business School and Curtin Business School can be read at https://bit.ly/2q8bOXF

- You had a clear sense of what was required from you
- Goals, expectations or targets were communicated to you
- You took direction from a boss or manager
- You had some sort of routine in the form of set working hours and breaks

Learnings from a cheese factory

The last time I was an employee I was 14-years-old (child labor was allowed back then!) and I worked in a cheese factory near my house. My job, as a warehouse operator, was to unpack large shipments of cheese and store them safely.

I'll never forget that job, and not because I enjoyed lugging 40lbs blocks of cheese around a freezing cold warehouse. No, what's burned into my mind is my place as a small cog in that big machine. My role was clearly defined and it never changed.

I knew exactly what was required from me: I had a target number of cheeses to unpack per hour, there was a supervisor keeping a close eye to make sure I met my target and, every day, I stuck to the same time schedule.

If the factory had tried to run any other way, it would have failed. Imagine if I'd been able to turn up whenever

I wanted, could do as much cheese shifting as I felt like and had no one to report to. I'll make an educated guess that, as a 14-year-old, I probably wouldn't have been found diligently working under my own steam.

Somehow, in the context of the cheese factory, it's easy to understand why guidelines, boundaries and processes were essential. In our own businesses, however, it's much harder to accept.

Both employees and entrepreneurs can fall foul of failure by freedom. Do not mistake this for laziness; this is a failure to recognize what humans need to be productive.

The happy medium between the desire for freedom and the need for boundaries is difficult to find because everyone needs slightly different things to work at their optimum, but the basics are the same.

Successful people even designate 'free' time

I mentor several entrepreneurs who are desperate to achieve success and conquer their goals. A handful of those seem committed to their ideas, but are way too relaxed. They drift from task to task with no plan, no hard deadlines and no implications if they don't deliver.

They call me up, tell me they're nearby right now and ask if I have an hour for a coffee. I can never spare an hour because every hour is accounted for. I plan everything I do.

If you can drop everything and meet for an impromptu coffee, chances are you're not being as productive as you could be and you need more structure. Successful people rarely leave things open and flexible.

'They' say if you want something done, give it to a busy person. Busy people are masters and mistresses of time management because they have little choice but to use every minute wisely. They cannot afford to be distracted.

It takes determination, self-discipline and training to overcome failure by freedom. When you start a business, that liberating feeling of having escaped the nine to five grind and being your own boss is a cocktail that can overpower even rational process-driven people.

So what do you do? If there is no immediate incentive to progress for short-term gain and no real deadlines, then you must manufacture urgency: create deadlines, timetable work, set goals and find ways to hold yourself accountable.

How to be the architect of your working week

1. Write a job description for yourself

If, like me, you were delighted to leave behind all the formal corporate processes big companies love when you became an entrepreneur, you might shudder at the thought of writing a job description for yourself, but bear with me.

Taking the time to think clearly about your role in your company might seem basic, but many of us never stop to do it, and it can really help to keep us focused on the core things we need to do.

Before I took this step, I'd never really thought too much about what I did every day, preferring to flip between different challenges as they came up. The problem was, I wasn't working on the right things. As soon as I thought about what I should be doing every day and wrote it down, it all seemed to fit into place. I would arrive at my office every day knowing clearly what it is I should be doing, and more importantly what I shouldn't.

2. Create a routine that suits your productivity highs and lows

As covered in the earlier chapter on self-awareness, we can achieve more in less time by knowing when we work best, and when we're pretty useless.

In many traditional jobs, our daily routine is shaped by our employers, but entrepreneurs have the luxury of being able to design a weekly routine that matches their workload to their productivity levels, with fantastic results.

To do this, you must map out your productivity peaks and troughs, and look at what factors improve your focus, be that caffeine, background noise, total silence, or the pressure of deadlines. Revisit Chapter One to follow the steps towards greater self-awareness before plotting your ideal work week.

3. Use your calendar to timetable your week

The humble calendar app is, in my opinion, one of the most under-utilized tools available to an entrepreneur who wants to achieve more without working harder.

A calendar should double up as a to-do list. As tasks present themselves, block off time to complete a specified job and set alerts and reminders for added time pressure.

By using your calendar as a to-do list, you're more likely to be ruthless about what can be scrapped and what makes it into the calendar - because the limits of your time are right there in front of you, in black and white. It forces you to protect your time from being used for non-essential tasks.

A word of warning. It can be tempting to fill your calendar with six, seven or even more tasks per day.

You'll quickly realize that it's only possible to do between one and three tasks to a high standard every day. For this to work, it's crucial to establish your pace as soon as you can, and to be realistic.

4. Create your own accountability

One study found that people are 65 percent more likely to meet a goal after committing to another person. That figure increases to 95 per cent when they build in ongoing meetings with someone who can check on their progress. The sheer act of someone else being involved with your goal or objective is enough to hugely boost your chances of completing it[28].

As entrepreneurs, we can use this powerful psychology hack to beat freedom failure and procrastination.

Share your objectives, and your calendar, with the people around you and you have an added incentive to deliver what you've set out to. It also helps us to feel connected, less isolated and more supported. My calendar has been public for years, and people on my

---

[28]Study by The American Society of Training and Development, as reported by Entrepreneur

team still seek me out to offer their help with what I'm working on.

Otherwise, grab a coffee and run through your calendar with your business partner or assistant. If you've got a team, try a daily meeting. At Time Etc, every day starts with a 'huddle' when we each share a success from yesterday and choose a new challenge for today. It's hugely popular, and a great example of how peer-to-peer accountability can drive a company forward.

CHAPTER SEVEN

KNOWING WHAT TO WORK ON

"All we have to decide is what to do with the time that is given to us."
– *Gandalf the Grey*

Let me take you back to 3am on a summer Sunday. I'm 21 and about four years into my first business. At that time on a Sunday morning, many twenty-somethings are still out partying somewhere. Not me. I'm at work, desperately trying to get through my to-do list so I can go to sleep.

This wasn't an isolated incident. Back then, long stints working through the night, fuelled by strong black coffee and energy drinks, was normal for me. This didn't just happen on occasion, this was every single day.

When my family and friends noticed I was exhausted, I told them it wasn't possible to stop because I had too much to do. Sound familiar?

My work pattern carried on for years until I met a guy called Dan.

Dan had started a very similar business to mine. He was the same age, we were targeting the same sort of customers, and he'd had the same start: neither of us had taken any investment and we'd both built our businesses alone from a single computer to a sizeable enterprise.

But somehow Dan had built a web hosting business that was twice the size of mine, and he didn't work all night.

Dan ended up selling his business to a major company and, in his new position as CEO, bought mine too, for less than half the money that he sold his business for.

You can probably imagine how that made me feel. I ended up thinking about it a lot. It bothered me so much, I decided to work out exactly how Dan had done it.

Eventually, I realized a few things about Dan:

    a) When it came to work, he was a machine. He very rarely, if ever, started a day wondering "where will this day take me?".

b) Dan was incredible at delegating and he always had people around him to do stuff.
c) Dan seemed to have an in-built sense of what tasks were important, and what wasn't worth his time and energy.

When I asked him how he knows what to work on, his answer was so simple it hurt: "I set a goal that I want to achieve. Then I don't do anything if it doesn't directly help me hit that goal". He described it as "kind of like a compass but the needle is pointing to my goal".

This was a complete contrast to how I was working. I had no goals other than "to grow bigger". Because of this, I had no compass to help me decide what to work on.

I did have a few long-term plans – like trying to build a new website – but I'd end up getting side-tracked almost every day by other tasks that seemed more urgent.

On top of that, I kept having new ideas. It became almost an addiction to play with these ideas instead of working on things that really mattered. A new phone system here, a new ticket system there. Every day I'd end up being busy, but not on things that actually helped me get the business to where I wanted it to be.

After dissecting how Dan had achieved more than me, I was determined to never make the same mistakes again. I wanted a high-growth business and I wanted to know I was working on the right things, so I developed a framework.

This framework has helped me to grow my own business by 400% over the past few years while working 35 hours a week. Since adopting it, there hasn't been a single day when I've been unclear about what to work on. Instead, the crucial tasks that I need to do every day are obvious to me, because they're linked to my overall goal.

Adopt this framework and you will be on a fast track to achieving more, without working any harder.

THE SCOOP

The Hard Work Myth wins when you can't figure out what you should be working on now, and what tasks should be delegated, binned or saved for later. There's only one way to tackle a sprawling list of things to do, work harder! But learn how to be selective, and you'll waste no time or energy.

Why goal setting hasn't worked for you

Goals work. There's a reason that entrepreneurs with investors breathing over them work so intensively. They are being held accountable by a higher, better-funded power. But goals also keep us focused and, by making and hitting them, we can define our success and grow faster.

Goal setting focuses the mind and steers you, mentally, towards your target in a way that nothing else can. The clever part is that a lot of this work happens behind the scenes, completely out of your conscious thought.

Slowly but surely, your goal will help to shape the little decisions you make every day. You'll suddenly stop wasting time on activities that you know or sense won't take you closer to your goal. You'll start to look critically at what you're devoting time to, and you ask pertinent questions like: Should I really be doing this now? Who could do this for me and do it better? What would I be doing if I wasn't doing this task? Am I allowing myself to be distracted?

Think of your goal as the destination in your sat-nav. It's much easier to plan your journey if you enter the end point before you set out, not when you're halfway there.

So far, so basic. But, while setting a goal might seem like a very simple thing to be suggesting in a book designed for entrepreneurs to achieve more in less time, I am stunned almost every week by the lack of goal setting among the 15,000+ entrepreneurs I have assisted and mentored.

I've discovered two main reasons that goal-setting ultimately fails:

- Firstly, we set huge, lofty and unrealistic goals which end up being demotivating. "I want to be in 100 countries" is a big, unfocused, scary goal.

- Secondly, we don't keep our goals in our minds as we run our businesses, so our day to day work and the tasks we're accomplishing don't directly contribute to hitting that goal.

It sounds simple, but these two principles are why many of us will never reach the goals we set, transforming them from valuable motivators to, at worse, powerful demotivators.

The only goals you'll ever need

That's why you need two goals: a BIG goal and a NOW goal.

Your big goal is your strategic vision, your long-term ambition. For me, it's growing my business to $100 million revenue.

My big goal reminds me where we're going with this business and how much further we've got to go. It reminds me that I'm trying to build a large, sustainable business that employs thousands of people and will be around for generations to come. It helps me justify investments in the best people and systems because I know they'll need to scale with the business as it grows.

What my big goal doesn't do, however, is show me how I'm going to get there. In fact, I have absolutely no idea how to grow our revenue to $100 million.

That's where my 'now goal' fits in. This is a goal that's attainable within the next few months e.g. to amplify marketing and advertising with a hard-hitting social media campaign, to double the sales team, or to secure five new clients.

The only rules are that this goal must be directly contribute to achieving your big goal and it must be quantifiable, such as a revenue figure, an increase in customers, or a sales target, that can function as a clear marker of success.

Now that you've set your goals, write them down somewhere and keep them visible at all times. This is crucial.

Next, write down five things you should do every week to achieve your now goal.

Here's my example:

My NOW goal: To get Time Etc to $10 million annual revenue within five to 10 years

My five things list:
1. Check new sales, upgrades and downgrades data so I know where we're at
2. Do at least one thing to increase client retention
3. Do at least one thing to drive new potential customers
4. Do at least one thing to improve conversion rate on our website
5. Write or produce at least one piece of content for our client base

Based on my list, my typical day consists of only performing tasks and executing ideas that I believe or know will help us to achieve our revenue goal, like increasing our customer retention and finding new and successful ways to nurture our clients, make them happy, and keep them loyal.

Next, control what you work on

When I first asked Dan how he achieved more than me, it felt like he just instinctively knew what to work on and when. He seemed to spend all of his time on high-value tasks and never appeared to be reacting to urgent or low-value tasks, despite plenty of those coming up on a regular basis.

I assumed Dan possessed superhuman levels of control and self-discipline but, in fact, he had developed a simple system that helped him stay focused: he created a buffer for his tasks and ideas, rather than trying to execute them as soon as they appeared.

You can do this too. Create a 'holding pen' in which to drop in all new tasks and ideas as soon as you think of them. This could be a list in a notebook, or an online document. Crucially, this is not your to-do list.

Many of us have a natural instinct to respond to tasks and ideas as they come up: we've all had days when we've set out to accomplish something big, only to be completely blindsided by an urgent-sounding email that's taken us down a completely different path.

Dan's method acts as a filter and a decision-making tool, catching everything that comes in so nothing important is forgotten.

Next, schedule time to go through your tasks and ideas list once a month or so and apply the following questions to each idea on your list:

- Would doing this task or developing this idea directly help me hit my goal?
- Does this task or idea fit with my top five list of things to focus on?
- Will something bad happen if I don't do it?

These questions will help you to extract only the tasks and ideas that really help you achieve your goal. These are the ones that you should be working on personally, either now or later.

For any tasks and ideas that don't meet these criteria, you have two options, either delegate them to someone else or get rid of them altogether.

Being selective and prepared to reject ideas and tasks is a productivity skill, but one that many people struggle to learn without better understanding themselves, and recognizing they are distracted.

Why is it so important?

When you study very successful people – ranging from entrepreneurs to celebrities to scientists – it becomes clear that being selective is an obvious component in their success.

Movie stars are often extremely selective over the films that they'll make, despite receiving piles of scripts and tons of offers at the peak of their careers.

Scientists cannot cure pancreatic cancer in the morning, Parkinson's after lunch, and solve the world's antibiotic immunity crisis in their spare time, or even do all this in a lifetime. They must specialize.

The length of your to-do list and the number of creative ideas you have in a week isn't a badge of honor. As a leader, you should be trying to do as few tasks as possible, but do them really well.

Therefore, it's important to think about your true capacity to get things done. I work on the basis that I can only complete two to three tasks a day, sometimes even fewer.

To decide what YOU should work on, use Eisenhower's technique

In a 1954 address, then-President Dwight D. Eisenhower quoted these words which he said were "a dilemma of modern man":

"I have two kinds of problems, the urgent and the important. The urgent are not important, and the important are never urgent."

Thus, Eisenhower is credited with the creation of a simple four-square grid, said to have improved his efficiency. Called the Eisenhower Matrix – or sometimes the Urgent Important Matrix – it involves taking every item on your to-do list and plotting it onto a grid, to help a busy person decide what to tackle first, what to delegate and what not to waste time on.

These are the rules:

Urgent and important: Do it yourself, and do it right now
Important, not urgent: Do it yourself, but schedule it for later
Urgent, not important: Delegate or outsource to someone else
Not urgent and not important: Eliminate it

URGENT AND IMPORTANT	IMPORTANT BUT NOT URGENT
DO NOW	**DO LATER**
URGENT BUT NOT IMPORTANT	NOT URGENT OR IMPORTANT
DELEGATE OR OUTSOURCE	**ELIMINATE**

The reason this presidential productivity method is so useful is because urgent tasks can quite easily push the important ones to the bottom of the pile.

Hacking up a to-do list, applying a liberal dose of ruthlessness, and putting it through this stress test before taking any action is a good way to make sure no time is wasted on tasks that are a) irrelevant or b) something that someone else could be doing, and possibly doing better.

We are naturally inclined to move on the urgent tasks first, before tackling the quick and easy bits that offer small bursts of satisfaction with every strike-through. But this approach distracts us from the big, important, and often complex, stuff.

Finally, learn how to deal with 'great' ideas

Something else I noticed about Dan was that he was never distracted by the latest 'big idea'. In fact, he didn't seem to talk about ideas very much at all, despite being one of the most innovative people I know. This surprised me.

As entrepreneurs, we try to solve problems and plug gaps in the market. You don't do those things unless you are naturally curious and unless ideas for resolving pain points you've identified flow freely.

Because of that, many entrepreneurs may feel their brains are hardwired for ideas generation, but it's vitally important to know when and where to apply ideas in your business, and what to discard.

Ideas are incredibly distracting, never fully formed, and prone to fizzling out. The mistake lots of creative people make is to treat tasks and ideas as one and the same.

Part of the problem is that ideas are really exciting, especially when you're feeling a bit stuck and they seem like an obvious solution to the problem you're facing, or if you feel like you want to be distracted from a task that's complex or boring.

To know whether executing your ideas are worth your time and effort, put them through this three-stage stress test to see how they stand up to scrutiny.

The idea stress test

1. Destroy the idea

Prove it won't work, or isn't needed, and you'll either end up with an idea that is even stronger or you'll know not to waste your time. At Time Etc we thought one of the best ideas we'd ever had was to create a bespoke video conferencing tool for our virtual assistants and clients to communicate through. But with a market already saturated with existing tools, building our own would have been a waste of time. Even so, at the time of having the idea, it really felt like this should have been an urgent priority for our business.

2. Give it time

If you sit on a good idea and let your subconscious mull it over, things emerge that weren't there when it first came to you.

Having attended a Facebook conference on virtual reality, I came away desperate to join the bleeding edge. I wanted to use VR to create meaningful connections between our virtual assistants and clients who are often many miles apart and unlikely to ever meet in person.
The time test solved this one: years on and VR is struggling to make waves beyond the gaming industry, and especially in the business world. This would have been a major distraction for us had we moved on it already. This one is now in the 'distant future' ideas file.

3. Improve it

It probably took me five years to know for sure that my own business was a good idea. It started as very unscalable – with full-time virtual assistants based in an office – before morphing again into the scalable model it is today with hundreds of freelance virtual assistants based all over the world.

You can improve an idea during the execution, or you can try to improve it before you start, which is a far superior plan of action. Sharing your idea with people you trust, including your team, because they already know your business, is recommended.

The iPhone has taught us that improving upon original ideas never really stops. Apple's smartphone is a cracking example of an idea that has withstood the test of time, and which continues to be iterated, arguably taking a step closer to perfection every year.

Be rough with your ideas to prove they're worth your time

This three-stage stress test is not dissimilar to the invention process. As British inventor Sir James Dyson said: "When you're experimenting, you'll often have one idea at the start of the design process, and arrive at a completely different one by the end." That's what you're looking to do. If your initial idea really was strong enough, it will withstand.

But many ideas *are* destined for improvement. The mouthwash Listerine started life on the shelf as an antiseptic, sold as both floor cleaner and gonorrhea treatment. But it wasn't a runaway success until it was marketed as a remedy for bad breath.

Many of us have ideas every day but very few of us handle them in a meaningful way. Be rough with your ideas, challenge them, break them, sit on them and mull them over.

CHAPTER EIGHT

DECONSTRUCTING DELEGATION

"It's easier to do it myself."
– Unknown failed entrepreneur

Penni Pike served as Sir Richard Branson's closest assistant for some 31 years after the charismatic English businessman poached her from Virgin's finance division in 1975. For the past decade, she's been the special advisor to my company, Time Etc.

Keen to understand more about how the Virgin empire was built, and Penni's role in it, I asked her to tell me some stories about her incredible career.

She recalled: "I was working from a small, dark and damp cramped room in Richard's houseboat which was moored on the canal at Little Venice. Despite appearances, the houseboat was very much the nerve center for a rapidly expanding Virgin group and the 10 telephones on my desk took up pretty much all of the space."

Penni continued: "One particularly cold autumn morning one of the phones rang, as it did throughout the day and night, and I answered. It was a lawyer called Randolph Fields who said he had started an airline and wanted to see if Richard would be interested in buying into it for £1.

"I immediately knew that Richard would be and wasted no time in setting up a call between Randolph and Richard. The rest, as they say, is history. Virgin Atlantic commenced its operations a short while later and is now one of the world's best-known multi-billion-dollar revenue airlines."

I asked Penni how Richard could trust her to know what was important and what wasn't out of the hundreds of calls she was fielding for him daily, and she explained: "Richard's approach to delegation is just to trust people. From the very first day I worked with him, there was never any doubt as to whether or not I could fulfil my role. When I left the finance division at Virgin we'd never worked together before and I had no official training, but he chose to trust me."

Most of us view having an assistant as a luxury, perhaps something we'd consider after having become successful. This is a big mistake. Many of the most successful high-profile entrepreneurs recruited an assistant at an embryonic stage in their journey.

Successful entrepreneurs understand assistants aren't a luxury or status symbol, they are a fundamental requirement to being able to achieve more.

Could this be a major factor in what makes some people successful and others not so? I think so. Delegating in business gives you a competitive advantage: in short, there's more time to focus on the 'big stuff' if you hand over the jobs you don't need to be doing yourself. And yet, it's a problem for millions of people.

THE SCOOP

Delegation is one of the hardest skills to master, particularly as many entrepreneurs need to be in control. But there are countless tasks that need doing that are not worth your time and effort. Anything that doesn't contribute to the growth of your business or take you closer to your goals must be delegated, or the Hard Work Myth will perpetuate.

Everyone knows that successful leaders must delegate, but many find it hard or impossible to do. If you've fallen for The Hard Work Myth you might find yourself saying things like "I'm too busy to delegate" or "they wouldn't do it as well as me anyway". It seems easier to simply work harder ourselves.

Gary Vaynerchuk, the high-profile founder of Vayner Media, has a strong view on this, and blames ego. He said: "If you can learn to let go and realize that most work is not that important, it becomes a hell of a lot easier to let someone else do it. Recognize that not every task requires your skill level and understanding; some tasks are perfectly doable by the multitude of bright, interesting people you hired. It's all about humility. Ego is the number one issue people can run into with delegation. Even though I have a ton of ego, I have a boatload more of humility than you think."[29]

Since 2007 when I founded Time Etc, I have seen first hand the power of delegation. Our clients have delegated more than 2 million tasks to our network of virtual assistants. It's pretty sobering to realize that this has given our clients back 57 years (and counting) to spend with their loved ones and to focus on growing their businesses.

Over the years, I've witnessed everything on the scale, from expert delegators, to whom it all comes easily, to

---

[29]You can read the full article on Gary Vaynerchuk's website

people who have really struggled to hand over work, despite having good intentions to change their working habits for the better when signing up.

Through studying some of the world's most successful entrepreneurs and the habits of our clients over the years, I've discovered five pillars that will make your delegation efforts a breeze.

The five pillars of delegation

Pillar 1: Delegate the right stuff

The single biggest reason that new delegators get their fingers burned is because they don't pass over the right tasks. I learned this lesson through my own painful experiences.

When I started Time Etc I decided it was time to figure out delegation once and for all. After all, if I was going to run a company that expected clients to delegate, I'd better be an expert at it.

So, I delegated *everything*. At home I hired people to do the cleaning, lawn mowing and even driving. At work I passed over almost all of my responsibilities including sales, marketing and leading our team.

There is no doubt I saved a lot of time this way. Most of these tasks were done fairly well by others and I was free to focus on whatever I liked. However, things soon started to unravel. People suddenly started quitting, and there was an air of unhappiness in the office. I had delegated too much.

It sounds silly now, but it took me months to realize that handing the leadership reins over to someone else was a terrible choice. People wanted me to lead them. They wanted direction from the person who had hired them.

They expected me to be present. Delegating these vital responsibilities had caused a huge motivation issue in the team. It was no-one's fault other than mine, and it caused plenty of damage.

At Time Etc we will often turn away potential clients who want to delegate vital parts of their business – such as finding new customers – because we know that, in a small business, there are absolutely some tasks that you must do yourself to succeed. To expect someone else to have the same care, attention and passion as you on a key task linked to the success of your business is flawed.

Pillar 2: Good enough is good enough

The fear of tasks not being done perfectly is a major driver in putting people off delegating in the first place and a leading cause of perceived "failure" when it goes wrong. However, seasoned delegators *expect* tasks not to be done perfectly and, in fact, they embrace it.

Not only do they accept tasks may not be done perfectly but, more often than not, they'll use this knowledge to carefully select the kind of tasks they delegate - picking low value but time-consuming tasks rather than tasks that are of critical importance.

Shark Tank's Barbara Corcoran wrote on Twitter: "I delegate everything I don't like to somebody else and realize that a job done 80% as well as you would do it, is good enough."

Remember, this is less about trying to force a critical task through the process of perfection and more about getting low-value non-critical tasks done fairly well.

Pillar 3: Be prepared to muck in

The very best painters and decorators know that 90% of the job is preparation, and just 10% is applying the paint. With delegation, the same principle applies.

Good preparation is key to improving the quality of what you get back once you've delegated a task. Take the time to document exactly what you want done, make sure they fully understand what it is you want them to do and clearly communicate your expectations.

Many people that struggle to delegate want to hand over tasks, save time and expect to receive a polished piece of work at the end. This is a near impossibility.

Successful delegators make their expectations very clear and are happy to answer questions in order to help get the task done. Rather than seeing requests for help as a failure in the delegation process, they see it as an opportunity to finesse the outcome.

Actually, the worst delegators can be really good at this, too. If you're a self-confessed control freak, and you're on hand to shape and improve the way a task you've set gets done, you'll probably feel far more comfortable about handing it over.

Pillar 4: Only expect a 25% return

Many of us do something very strange when we delegate work. We expect that:

a) We'll never have to touch that task again. Once it's gone, it's entirely the responsibility of the person doing it. We've handed it over, now it's theirs not ours.
b) We'll save the exact amount of time we think a task would have taken us to complete. So, if we think writing a blog might take two hours, we expect to save a full two hours by delegating.

Neither of these statements is true.

Seasoned delegators know that even when you hand over a task they're still fully responsible for it. In reality, you're only lending it to them. You're still going to need to be fully invested in the task, available to answer questions and perhaps even contribute to the completion of the task yourself. Delegating is just one step in a delicate dance of collaboration to get a task finished. They know the act of delegation isn't the end of the story.

Expert delegators also know they will normally only save a small amount of time on each task they hand over. This is always true at the start of a new delegating relationship and often remains true even when two people have worked together for a long time.

One-hour task → Novice delegator expects they'll save one hour

One-hour task → Pro delegator expects they'll save 15-20 minutes

When you delegate a task that would have taken you an hour to complete yourself, by the time you've delegated it, offered guidance, assisted with queries and perhaps even helped to complete the task yourself you'll only save a small fraction of the time it would have taken you to do the task.

The key is that as long as you're saving *some* time, you're winning - and successful delegators use this to their advantage. Rather than seeing it as a failure that they've spent 40 minutes delegating a one-hour task, they see it as a success that they've still saved 20 minutes.

Let's take an example from my company. I work with a talented marketing assistant called Harriet and one of her jobs is to help me create a weekly video where I'll tackle a particular business or productivity challenge[30]. It takes about an hour of prep, an hour for filming and a further hour for editing to put one of our videos together.

It's logical, therefore, to think that I should be able to save at least two hours for each video because I've delegated all responsibility to Harriet, but this isn't the case. I have to provide direction on the content, help to solidify each idea, be available for filming and give feedback on edits.

The end result is that I probably save an hour in total but I am very happy with that saving - it's a whole hour I wouldn't otherwise have if I was doing the task myself.

And, of course, the more tasks you delegate, the more time you save.

---

[30]Curious?! You can watch our videos at timeetc.com

Pillar 5: Bestow instant trust

Normally, trust is earned over time. But here's some news for you: in business there is absolutely zero time for trust-building in that way - and Penni Pike's story teaches us that.

The secret is this: to get the very best out of people, take a leap of blind faith and give your trust them before it's been earned. In other words, create trust by declaring (and meaning) it.

This has an almost magical effect on the person you're delegating to. They feel empowered, responsible and accountable, meaning they're more likely to do their best work.

How to know what to delegate

Have you ever considered that you might not be the best person to complete the many tasks on your to-do list?

Some of the most of the most brilliant business people of our time will tell you that delegation is central to their success because they've learned what not to do themselves.

In the New York Times, Sir Richard Branson wrote: "When I try a new task and find it's not my cup of tea, or I'm simply not cut out to do it, I delegate it to someone who is passionate about the work, knowing that person will do a great job."[31]

Branson explains that when he started Virgin, he lacked vital knowledge in accounting and wasn't good with numbers, and so hired an accountant - which you might well have done yourself. From that experience, he realized delegating held the key to growth.

Putting your faith in others, while making yourself available to help them, might just be the best business move you ever make.

In the previous chapter we looked at how the Eisenhower Matrix can help you decide what tasks you should perform yourself. It also helps you decide what to delegate i.e. anything that's urgent but not important.

If the Eisenhower Matrix isn't for you, try the bucket technique.

Imagine a bucket that's holding all of the tasks that really matter to you or your business. These are the things that you want and need to take great care of,

---

[31]You can read the full article here https://bit.ly/2BfVWF4

such as redesigning a website or meeting an important client.

The bucket is already pretty full, now top it up with all the things that aren't vitally urgent but need to be done, such as reading emails, calling back various suppliers or job candidates. The bucket's contents is now spilling over the sides. Only the things at the top of the bucket will ever spill over – the non-critical tasks – leaving the vital tasks safely in the bucket for me to complete myself.

To maximize my chances of delegating the right tasks, I also choose the repetitive tasks that I would otherwise find myself doing all the time. Delegate them once and I benefit from them being done by someone else time after time. The math doesn't lie: saving just 20 minutes a day through delegating saves me a total of 76 hours over a year.

CHAPTER NINE

HIRING HURTS

"I'd rather interview 50 people and not hire anyone than hire the wrong person."
– Jeff Bezos

Picture this scene. It's half-past nine in the evening and I'm the last person left in the office.

I'm in the women's toilets where the floor is flooded with murky brown water and the air stinks.

Earlier that day, a member of our team had blocked the toilet. Unfortunately, her panicked, frantic attempts to flush the blockage had caused a colossal flood.

I could hardly delegate this unhappy task to one of my team so, it fell to me, the business owner, to fix the problem.

As I pushed at the blockage with a plunger, I was plagued by the realization that hiring a small team had caused me more work, worry and hassle than it had ever saved me.

Employees were supposed to have made my life simpler but, here I was, late at night, desperately attempting to dislodge someone's poop from a U-bend instead of enjoying an evening at home with my family.

I managed to see the funny side, but unblocking that toilet also served as a wake-up call. I made a promise that night that I would *never* hire again without *really* needing to.

I'm aware this is a controversial point of view, but it's one I'm passionate about. Far from saving time for small business owners, hiring your first few employees can in fact consume pretty much all of it.

THE SCOOP

Don't confuse hiring with delegation. You can delegate most tasks to virtual assistants and freelance consultants without taking on the risk of hiring. In fact, hiring too early fuels The Hard Work Myth. Although it feels like more employees supporting you should make life easier, hiring always involves a lot more time and effort than many realize, and it changes your job description whether you like it or not. Put off hiring until all other avenues – including freelancers and automation software – and are exhausted first.

Over the years, I've recruited hundreds of employees, and refined a number of techniques designed to attract, manage, motivate and retain those people. These days, brilliant coaches and managers help look after, manage and motivate my team, yet I still find it challenging.

I know I'm not alone. My company, Time Etc, works with small business clients. Some of them use our virtual assistants *before* making their first hire. I've lost count of the number of clients who have hired their first full-time employee, stopped using their virtual assistant, and then, several months later, come back to us and asked for their VA back because their hire has gone wrong.

Why? Because hiring demands a whole new set of skills on top of learning to delegate.

When I started the business, it was me and two other co-founders, Vic and Fran. For months we shared ideas, planned and developed strategies on how the business would function and grow.

I spent my days, and some nights, coding our platform, building it from scratch at my leisure. Life as an entrepreneur then was exciting, enjoyable and fairly straightforward.

That all changed when we started to hire. For months, I'd had a burning desire to build a team because it felt like that would signal to others that we were a 'proper' business. So one day, without pausing to think, I started interviewing.

Employing people seen as a badge of honor. People commented that we must be doing well as we were hiring. It was nice to hear those endorsements, though I see now they weren't based on fact.

It also felt good to be able to recruit a few brilliant and talented local people to join us on our journey. We leased an office to accommodate our growing team and set about turning it into the best place to work.

Fast forward a few short months and things were not going so well. The business had failed to pick up as many new customers as we had anticipated. Suddenly $26,000 a month needed to be budgeted for payroll and we were running low on funds.

Added to that, our small and initially enthusiastic team didn't have enough to do and, as a result, employees were demotivated. I could keep myself motivated, but I didn't know the first thing about how to inspire other people, which meant we were dealing with people issues left right and center.

My day was now consumed with juggling the finances, firefighting and in meetings with our team. Developing our platform and growing the business fell by the wayside.

I had totally failed to predict that, by making the decision to bring employees into our business, my role would have to change.

I'd gone from having the freedom to be creative and do what I loved – coding – and morphed into a reluctant and underprepared full-time manager. Suddenly I had to provide constant direction, instruction and motivation and I was completely unprepared.

My financial security had gone from perfect to being compromised, and the relationship between us co-founders was strained as a result.

In the end, we ended up losing most of that team within a couple of years. It took about six years to find and be able to afford team leaders that would finally let me employ and retain a team while I focused on the things I really wanted to, like product development.

Hiring is inevitable for most businesses, especially those that undergo rapid growth. I'm not saying you shouldn't aim to hire people. Being able to provide talented people with a great place to work and a real career is surely one of the hugely rewarding aspects of being an entrepreneur, but we shouldn't see it as the holy grail of company growth.

And, if possible, we should delay the complexity, cost, regulation and commitment for as long as possible to give our businesses a fighting chance.

If I could go back, I would put off hiring for as long as possible and consider instead the many alternatives. Resisting hiring where possible has served my business well: our automated technology platform does much of the work and we have only 25 talented full-time staff running what is now a profitable international business.

I found to my cost that hiring early on doesn't reduce your workload but increases it, putting you further away from your goal of achieving more without working harder.

What happens when you hire?

Hiring is rather like the touch paper on a firework: once lit there's nothing you can do to stop it. As soon as you've agreed to hire your first employee, there's no stopping the following:

1. The dynamic changes for you. You switch roles from entrepreneur to manager. You go from having the freedom to do what you like to having serious HR obligations that, if not met, can cause big problems for your business.

2. You'll be expected to become an expert in people and understand their individual needs and motivations. You'll also be expected to make time for everyone, on a weekly or even daily basis. I found this really tough, on top of an already packed diary.

3. You will go from setting your own goals and keeping your motivation and energy up to having to do that for others as well. Early on, I struggled with knowing how to find goals that were actually motivating for my team.

4. You will have more mouths to feed. You go from ensuring you can survive financially to feeling completely responsible for the survival and financial security of your team and their families and, as best-selling author Simon Sinek says, "leaders eat last". You will feel the pressure of ensuring that, month after month, no matter what happens to your business, you cannot let them down. The scary reality of needing to pay salaries that people depend on can keep you awake at night.

It's harder than ever to keep employees

According to an analysis of resumés by Glassdoor – a website where employees can anonymously review companies and their management – the average worker is now spending only 15 months in a role[32]. And Gallup reports that 51% of American workers are ready to leave their current jobs[33].

Jobs and careers are no longer for life. As a small business owner, you can no longer assume the people you bring into the fold are going to be around in two years' time.

It's extremely difficult to motivate yourself to devote time and resources to training people up when you know that

---

[32]According to a Glassdoor survey here: https://bit.ly/2VOrKtZ
[33]Gallup's State of the American Workplace report: https://bit.ly/2xL6ae6

you're highly likely to have to replace that person very soon. And yet, that's what many of us do every day.

I have a friend called Mark who is an inspirational business leader. He is a well-known entrepreneur who has grown multiple businesses to tens of millions of dollars in revenue. His specialty is working with medium-sized businesses to help them expand overseas.

He has won multiple awards for building incredible cultures and great places to work. He has employed – directly or indirectly – thousands of people.

This guy practically wrote the book on culture, employment and growing businesses that people love to work for. And now he is in demand all over the world as a consultant that helps companies do the same.

A couple of years ago Mark set up a micro-business to run alongside his consultancy work, so he recruited a little team to work with him.

And can you guess what happened? He struggled. This guy who knew everything about happy company cultures experienced failure after failure as person after person came into his business and rapidly quit. I know this because, after yet another person left, Mark came to me and asked me to find him a virtual assistant to help.

Why did this happen? Because big businesses, like the companies Mark has either built or long worked with, had all the stuff you could ever need to attract and retain incredible people. Great teams to work with, established cultures and systems, beautiful offices, superb benefits packages, amazing salaries, you name it.

But when we go out on our own as small entrepreneurs, we may have none of those resources. It is simply much harder to attract the best people and retain them - especially if you've never done it before and the only unique selling point you can offer is 'greater responsibility and autonomy'.

If even Mark has found it almost impossible to hire successfully, what hope do the rest of us have?

Hiring may be the least efficient way to grow

When Phil Keeling started his plumbing business back in 2007, one of the first things he learned was that hiring full-time can be extremely inefficient.

Phil was snowed under with work and, to solve the problem, he hired an engineer, offering him a generous salary. To get him around town, he went out and leased and branded van for his new worker to use.

Before he knew it, Phil had a fleet of five vans and five engineers. For a little while, he had a thriving plumbing

The Hard Work Myth

business doing hundreds of jobs a month for happy customers. Until the following summer.

That year was one of the longest, warmest summers on record. Britain was in the grip of a prolonged heatwave which quickly put an end to Phil's expansion. With no one in the U.K. using their heating, work suddenly dried up for those five engineers. Phil was forced to act fast.

Nervous that he was going to have to lay people off, Phil approached his engineers and asked them if they'd agree to work with him on a freelance basis, sharing a much larger portion of the profits and leaving them free to fill in any gaps with their own jobs on the side. He would split the hourly fee that his clients paid him 50/50 with the engineers.

Thankfully, Phil's team stood behind him and, before long, they navigated out of the tight spot they found themselves in by working together.

When winter finally arrived, the engineers made more money for their families than they'd ever done before, and Phil was able to relax knowing when the next slow summer came, his business would continue to prosper.

What Phil learned here is that hiring people full-time in a small business is often the least financially sensible thing you can do because overheads always need to be met, even when sales dry up.

Unless you're taking a carefully calculated risk, having employees doing nothing, waiting for work to come in, is hugely wasteful to any business.

There are more good alternatives than ever before

It used to be that the only way you could find someone to help in your small business was to find someone local and employ them.

Now, we're spoilt for choice. In the past decade, there has been a revolution in how you can run and resource your small business with subscriptions and software platforms replacing big, inflexible overheads, like salaries (think Xero replacing bookkeepers).

When only human help will do, there are literally thousands of options available. Marketplaces like Freelancer.com and Elance.com are packed full of skilled people who will happily work for your business on a flexible and part-time basis to help you achieve more.

If you're looking for a way of getting administrative tasks done in your business, and life, with none of the risk and hassle of hiring, my company, Time Etc, will pair you with a highly-experienced virtual assistant who you'll get to know and trust, and we'll take care of all the finer details like payments too.

Happily, the freelance economy in the U.S. is thriving. An estimated 57.3 million Americans freelanced in 2017, which is 36% of the workforce, contributing approximately $1.4 trillion annually to the economy[34].

All that talent is on tap, waiting to be called upon. Small businesses can enlist the skills of literally millions of quality, experienced freelancers for a fraction of the cost of hiring.

Making use of the world's huge freelance talent pool means that you can focus on running your business without needing to become a full-time people manager or HR expert. You can continue to work from wherever you like, rather than having to get an office. You can flex your overheads up and down as you can afford to, rather than having to fund full-time salaries throughout the year.

What does this mean for you? Resource your business wisely and you'll be well on your way to achieving more, without working harder. The Hard Work Myth can be busted simply by tasking talented freelancers with the jobs you should have never been doing in the first place, and delegating expertly.

---

[34]According to a study of 6,000 U.S.workers conducted by independent research firm Edelman Intelligence and commissioned in partnership by Upwork and Freelancers Union (2017)

CHAPTER TEN

THE POWER OF THE TINY CHANGE

"I have not failed. I've just found 10,000 ways that won't work."
– Thomas A. Edison

I remember the very first time I hit The Wall. I was a teenager and only months into running my first business. To make it financially viable for me to continue, I needed to find 20 new paying customers every day.

The number of daily sign-ups had increased from two to five to eight to 10. But then it started to flatline.

My tactic was to advertise in print magazines, which meant a delay of several weeks between paying for an advertisement to appear and seeing a response. I would excitedly hold my breath for the uplift. Surely this latest campaign would be the one that got me to the 20 paying customers I needed?

It didn't. Nothing seemed to work. I ran ad after ad, using up a lot of the little money I had, and nothing happened.

I'm not the only one who has encountered a hurdle that seems impossible to overcome, whether it's increasing sales, driving your revenue past a certain point, or beating procrastination.

THE SCOOP

Problem solving is never about slogging your guts out. It's about intelligence, agility and the courage to try something new. The Hard Work Myth feeds off our belief that spending hours upon hours breaking down walls is the solution. Think about the last time you made a breakthrough in your business. How did you do it?

Every day, thousands of entrepreneurs around the world encounter hurdles. Clear these hurdles and you'll unlock growth, profits and success. Don't, and it might just be the end of your journey as an entrepreneur.

The odds are not stacked in our favor either: only 20.6% of first time entrepreneurs make it[35]. Worse still, a staggering 94% of companies will never hit $1M in annual revenue[36].

The secret is not to work harder

The really big problem with encountering walls is that they feed The Hard Work Myth. I know business owners who think they've overcome a major blockage with sheer hard work, but that is rarely the case.

The solution to my problem had nothing to do with the days I spent re-designing those print adverts or the long hours spent on the phone carefully negotiating for more advertising space, or even working for a month into the small hours on building a new website that would capture as many new customers as possible.

Actually, I made one very tiny change to my approach. A change that felt almost insignificant at the time.

The great power of tiny change

Instead of redesigning my adverts for the tenth time, I emailed both editors of the two magazines I was advertising in and asked them to write about my

---

[35]According to this very interesting 2006 paper about Skill vs. Luck in Entrepreneurship and Venture Capital: https://bit.ly/2piXCuL
[36]As cited by David Cummings here: https://bit.ly/23ELdL7

company. And it worked. Within just a couple of months, that press coverage helped me exceed my goal of 20 paying customers a day by 100%.

It was a valuable lesson: breaking down walls has absolutely nothing to do with striking them harder. In fact, I barely did any "work" to make it happen, short of firing off a couple of emails that took minutes to write. I just tried something different.

As an entrepreneur, you are absolutely guaranteed to face roadblocks repeatedly throughout your business career.

How you respond will dictate whether you succeed or not, and it will threaten the work-life balance you have worked so hard to create.

Problem solving is one of the best ways a business owner can spend his or her time, because every solution clears the way towards growth and success and helps you understand your business and customers a little bit more.

Successful business people are just good problem solvers

Look at some of the world's most successful people and you'll see they have two things in common, none of which involve working longer hours or working harder.

Don't get me wrong, grit, determination and perseverance do feature heavily in all success stories.

Milton Hershey started three unsuccessful candy companies before his fourth – the Lancaster Caramel Company – succeeded. His fifth business, The Hershey Company, of course, needs no introduction.

In the 1990s, author JK Rowling – whose 2019 net worth is estimated by The Sunday Times Rich List to be $911M – was famously turned down by 12 different publishers before Bloomsbury agreed to print the first Harry Potter manuscript. She wrote it while receiving welfare benefits during a dark period in her life.

But the ability to execute probable solutions with speed and bravery is also a trope.

Cable channel The Oprah Winfrey Network, led by the media mogul herself, struggled with an identity crisis after it launched in 2011, offering a below-par program line up to viewers keen to immerse themselves in Brand Oprah.

The initial plan was to offer factual shows themed around Winfrey's personal philosophy – 'living your best life' – covering topics like spirituality and health. But it wasn't until the network changed tack and targeted African American women with premium scripted dramas that OWN found its stride and became a ratings success.

And then there is business tycoon Sir Richard Branson, whose aim for Virgin Atlantic was to give passengers an unparalleled flying experience. He knew he could offer a service like no other, but he lacked knowledge of the industry. Still, he persisted and rented a Boeing 747 – Virgin's only plane – to complete a test flight.

But, during the flight, a flock of birds flew into the engine, causing extensive damage. The airline couldn't get certified to start carrying passengers without a working plane, and Branson didn't have the money to get it fixed.

At this point, many would have given up, but instead, he worked out a way around the problem. He restructured all of his companies and pulled money from other ventures to get the plane fixed. Thanks to his ability to find a solution, and action it, his airline got the certification it needed to make its first flight and it quickly became a huge success.

Of course, not every business is as well-resourced as Virgin. But businesses of all sizes are making tiny yet powerful changes all the time. Laura Jennings founded online gift store of KnackShops.com, which lets customers personalize their purchases.

She told me: "Two years ago the principle of my ad agency made an off-hand comment about her experience as a customer on my site: she said she loved the gift she created but 'was surprised at how many clicks it took'. I pondered that for a day or two and still couldn't make sense of it - 'lots of clicks' is not how our site works!

"So I asked her to come into the office and make a gift while my entire company silently observed. We were amazed – and embarrassed – by what we saw her do.

She was bypassing the 'obvious' path to pursue a much more convoluted process we had never even imagined someone might take. And if a brilliant digital native like her was using our site this way, what were other site visitors doing?"

The next day, Jennings and her team placed a sandwich board on the sidewalk outside their office. It read: *If you give us 10 minutes to test our site, we'll give you $20.*

She said: "Whenever someone would walk in to take us up on the offer, everyone in the company would drop what they were doing to silently observe the new person interacting with our site. When the visitor had left, we'd debrief and address whatever had confused them. We iterated like this for weeks, until visitor after visitor easily found the quickest path to creating something unique."

Matt Schmidt is CEO of Diabetes Life Solutions, which sells affordable life insurance to people with Type 1 and Type 2 diabetes. Two years ago, he noticed referral traffic from existing clients – which created some of its most profitable leads – was starting to drop off.

Schmidt told me: "Our head of marketing recommended that we offer to donate a portion of our commissions to a diabetes charity of the client's choice, if they'd recommend others in the diabetes community to us. A simple gesture like this turned around referral traffic by about 1000%."

Today, the company still donates 25% of its commissions to diabetes charities.

Kyra Schaefer, founder of As You Wish Publishing, a business dedicated to making book publishing accessible for aspiring authors, was experiencing a sales problem: she was undervaluing and underpricing her offering.

She recalled: "I would adjust my price based on how I felt the sales conversation was going. It came from a lack of confidence which showed up time and again. This lack of confidence resulted in me underpricing my service, which led to customers undervaluing my service, my time and my energy."

What did she do? "I did something so simple it was ridiculous. I shut up. Yes, once I asked for the sale, I shut my mouth. The silence gave my customer time to evaluate their options and think of questions. I would answer their follow-up questions but wouldn't lower my price."

Schaefer credits this simple strategy with taking her small company from barely getting by to turning over six figures a year.

Think about the tiny changes you've made in your business that have had a really big impact on usability, referrals or sales. Did they involve hours of hard labor, or creativity?

Note that working nights and weekends doesn't feature here. What these stories teach us is that curiosity and humility – to pinpoint problems and speedily test creative remedies – can put your business back on the path to growth. This agile approach – implementing tiny powerful changes without delay – is far more effective than flogging yourself. Don't believe the Hard Work Myth: it really does no one any favors.

CONCLUSION

I want to thank you for taking the time to read this book and, hopefully, for taking its message to heart. Because the Hard Work Myth deserves to be laid bare.

For decades it has been damaging health and hindering success without being called out.

Unpicking such a widely held belief is not easy when we are all products of a system that teaches us that success is dependent on hours worked.

That's why, to bust The Hard Work Myth, we must reprogram ourselves and our belief system.

You have to choose to ignore that great big lie spread by teachers, parents and employers, who don't know any better, that the more we work, the more we'll achieve.

Because if you don't, it will not only hamper your success, it could even ruin your life, like it almost ruined mine.

You can be a successful entrepreneur, achieve everything you want to *and* find plenty of time to watch your kids grow up and devote to nurturing your friendships and relationships.

The methods and principles we've covered in this book make this possible for you and me. They also happen to be the very same methods and principles already adopted by many of the world's most successful business folk.

I am living proof that it's possible to grow a multi-national business by 400%, selling almost $35 million worth of services, in a few short years with no external investment, all while working 35 hours a week or less.

All I've done is gain greater self-awareness, change my mindset, and put routines and structures in place to support that change.

If you're anything like I was, you've been fighting to achieve more for years. You know you're spending too long reading the news, that your inbox has become a distraction and that you should be delegating more.

You've tried working harder but it's not leading to greater success.

Your life has immense value. By failing to achieve all that you're capable of while working harder, you're undermining your own financial potential, as well as your health and wellbeing.

You have as much potential as any of the high profile ultra-successful entrepreneurs I've mentioned in this book, many of whom are billionaires.

But it's not really about the money. Imagine how your life would feel without the daily tussle between what you want to achieve and what's possible fitted around family, home and friends.

Imagine how you'd feel if you achieved everything you want at work and still managed to get home to tuck your kids in and read them a bedtime story.

Our routines and obligations weigh us down. And the 'knowledge' that floats around – like delegating is more hassle than it's worth or that no entrepreneur that's in it to win it should get the luxury of weekends – fast become truth.

Understanding that none of these things need to apply to you is key.

My personal experience is the more I have understood myself and what I need to achieve, the more I have achieved.

Tweaking how I think worked for me where traditional management techniques and fast 'productivity hacks' that are all over the internet did not.

As you've seen, achieving more by working less hard, oddly enough, requires immense discipline. To make a start right now, you can begin by questioning absolutely every task you're doing and becoming self-aware.

If nothing else, I hope that by reading this book you truly understand that with some quite small changes you can achieve success without sacrificing your life.

YOUR INVITATION

Thank you for taking the time to read the book. Now, it's time to start achieving more, without working harder.

A virtual assistant is an experienced executive assistant who chooses to work from home, on a part-time basis. So far, more than 15,000 entrepreneurs have discovered that working with one can be the secret to achieving much more every day, at a fraction of the cost of hiring a full-time assistant.

I want to help you to achieve your goals, to find balance and to grow a successful business without sacrificing your family and I invite you to try our virtual assistant service today.

To try a virtual assistant now, go to **www.timeetc.com/myth**

As well as discovering how incredible it feels to be supported by an assistant, you'll also find exclusive downloads, content and videos designed to help you achieve more, without working harder.

PLEASE SPREAD THE WORD

I found writing this book a massive challenge.

I'm not a natural writer and, in all, it's taken about 18 months of hard graft to put this together - with plenty of help along the way.

It would mean a huge amount to me if you could share the book. If you like it, please tell as many people as you can about it to help them gain access to the essential knowledge contained in this book. It might really help them.

To make things interesting, I'm offering the chance to win a virtual assistant for six months (worth $1500+). To enter, just post to Instagram, Facebook or Linkedin tagging it **#thehardworkmyth** and include a link to **hardworkmyth.com,** so people know where to get the book.

I'll be picking a new winner every six months, so keep your eye out for a message from me!

L - #0156 - 130220 - C0 - 210/148/9 - PB - DID2768326